PETER BROCK is a member of the Department of History at the University of Toronto.

The Slovaks lived under Hungarian rule for centuries, with no clear sense of political separateness, preserving Slovak as their spoken language, but using Czech as their written language. In the last decades of the 18th and the first half of the 19th centuries, the efforts made by clerical intellectuals to develop a language more closely attuned to Slovak needs led to the rise of Slovak nationalism.

*The Slovak National Awakening* describes three major stages in the development of national consciousness. In the 1780s Catholic intellectuals began to write in the vernacular; a Catholic priest, Bernolák, produced a Slovak grammar and dictionary and an influential treatise in defence of Slovak as a language separate from Czech. However, while Slovak ethnic distinctness was being asserted, the sense of belonging to the Hungarian nation was not questioned. The next steps were taken by the Protestant intelligentsia, who had been pro-Czech since the Reformation. Influenced by German concepts of linguistic nationalism, they began to assert Slovak cultural and linguistic separateness, but still within the political framework of the Hungarian state.

The third stage in the Slovak Awakening came in the mid-1840s when a group of young Protestant intellectuals, led by L'udovít Štúr, rejected their predecessors' 'Czechoslovakism' and advocated a Slovak language and a Slovak nationality. In 1851, the Catholic Bernolákites and the Protestant Štúrites were able to agree on the language that became the basis of modern Slovak.

This study of the relation between language and nationalism will appeal to specialists in European history and will also be of interest for the light it throws on modern separatist and anti-imperialist movements.

PETER BROCK

The Slovak
National Awakening:
an essay in the
intellectual history of
east central Europe

UNIVERSITY OF TORONTO PRESS
TORONTO AND BUFFALO

© University of Toronto Press 1976
Toronto and Buffalo
Printed in Canada

Library of Congress Cataloging in Publication Data

Brock, Peter, 1920-
  The Slovak national awakening.
  Bibliography: p.
  Includes index.
  1. Slovakia – History.   2. Nationalism – Slovakia.
  I. Title.
  DB666.B76      943.7'3      75-42013
  ISBN 0-8020-5337-8

126492

In Western Europe modern nationalism was
the work of statesmen and political leaders ...
In Central and Eastern Europe it was the poet,
the philologist, and the historian who created
the nationalities.

HANS KOHN

# Contents

# Preface

The Slovaks, a rural people, lived under Hungarian rule for a thousand years. Their history, therefore, is closely interwoven with that of the Magyars, who provided the ruling class of the old multicultural Hungarian state from its inception in the tenth century until its dissolution in 1918. When at the end of the eighteenth century the idea of modern nationalism spread from its birthplace in western Europe eastwards into central Europe, it underwent considerable change. Beside the original idea of the 'state-nation,' that is, the politically dominant nation in a state, there arose a second idea, that of the cultural-linguistic nation, whose proponents – to begin with at any rate – generally eschewed political objectives. Beyond the Rhine and the Alps numerous peoples whose names had not been seen on the political map of Europe for many centuries, or in some cases had never appeared on it at all, began to claim national identities. More accurately, their intellectual elites, at first often only at one or two removes from the village, began to put forward such claims.

The situation was complex. For instance, the emergent nationalism of the independent but politically fragmented Germans combined political aspirations to territorial unification with a cultural and linguistic renascence. Much the same may be said of the two largest nations of east central Europe, the Poles, whose state disappeared altogether in 1795, and the Magyars, who balanced uneasily between autonomy and dependence on their Habsburg ruler. Other peoples of the area, the Czechs, Serbs, and Croats as well as the Rumanians, were not without pretensions to state-nationhood, although during the first half of the nineteenth century their nationalism was in practice primarily cultural and linguistic. If we exclude the Lusatian Serbs (or Sorbs), a minute island of Slav speakers within a German sea, only the Slovenes and the Slovaks, who numbered over two million in the first half of the nineteenth century, produced a nationalism that long remained merely cultural and linguistic. The confrontation slowly developing after the end of the eighteenth century between the political, state-oriented nationalism of the Magyar landowning class and the cultural nationalism of the Slovak intellectual elite, spokesmen – albeit self-appointed – of a peasant people, resulted from two opposed ideas of nationality.

The following pages deal primarily with intellectual history. Their theme is the evolution of an idea, the Slovak idea of nationality. An economic or social historian would treat the history of Slovak nationalism differently, and so would a political historian, a literary historian, or a historian of language. I do not claim to have provided an exhaustive treatment of the awakening of Slovak cultural life; I have merely tried to outline the story down to the first public demands of a political nature made by the Slovaks in the spring of 1848. I can make no claim, either, to archival research and to the kind of intimate knowledge of the subject, acquired only by decades of study, that is found, for instance, in the works of historians of such dissimilar viewpoints as Rapant, Gogolák, and Butvin. In dealing with developments that are still highly controversial I have simply aimed at a reasonably accurate and objective account of an important subject on which scarcely any reliable literature exists in English.

For place-names with varying forms I have normally employed the form in current use (where an acceptable English version does not exist). This is purely for convenience and does not imply any political judgment in disputed cases.

I would like to thank the American Council of Learned Societies and the Centre for Russian and East European Studies at the University of Toronto for financial support in my research on this book, and also M. Jean Houston, executive editor of the University of Toronto Press, and Larry MacDonald, my editor, for valuable assistance at various stages in its production. I also wish to express my appreciation for the help received in a number of libraries, more especially the University Library in Bratislava and the Interlibrary Loan Service of the University of Toronto Library. This book has been published with the help of grants from the Social Science Research Council of Canada, using funds provided by the Canada Council, and from the Publications Fund of the University of Toronto Press.

PB

# THE SLOVAK NATIONAL AWAKENING

# 1
# The dawn of
# Slovak nationalism

A Slovak vernacular was first used for literary purposes in the 1780s when it replaced Czech among the Slovak Catholic intelligentsia.[1] Consciousness of separate identity, however, was much older. Divided from the Magyars and from the Germans of north Hungary by language and ethnic origin, from the Czechs by a political frontier, from the Poles by the physical barrier of the Carpathian range, and from the Ruthenians (Ukrainians) by religion, the Slovaks had long possessed at least a vague feeling that they were different from their neighbours. At the same time close ties existed tending to unite the Slovaks with these neighbouring peoples and to obscure that sense of otherness. A common state, and in respect to the upper classes a shared political tradition, had for many centuries embraced both the Slovak and the Magyar-speaking subjects of the Hungarian kingdom. Lutheranism joined many Slovaks and Germans in the same religious communion while setting them apart from those who spoke their own language yet professed a different faith. The church union of the mid-seventeenth century smoothed the way for Ruthenians and Slovaks to merge. Finally, Catholic as well as Protestant Slovaks used Czech as their literary language well into the eighteenth century, thus making it easy to conceive of a Czechoslovak unity. Even from more distantly placed Slav peoples the Slovaks often found it difficult to distinguish themselves with any degree of certainty. They usually called themselves simply 'Slavs,' or 'Slavs of Hungary' if they wished to be precise. On the other hand, the term 'Slovak' could be used to designate Slavs in general. This nomenclature survived into the nineteenth century.

The Slovak countryfolk of course had spoken their own dialects from time immemorial. The Old Slavonic literature produced in Slovakia in the period of the Great Moravian state and after its fall preserved faint traces of the impact of Slovak vernacular speech. However, Hungarian rule of the country beginning in the tenth century eventually brought the exclusive sway of written Latin. Not until the fifteenth century do we find a Slavonic vernacular in use again (its use may indeed have begun in the previous century though nothing has survived of that date). But this was the Czech language, not a form of Slovak, and it was adopted chiefly for legal and administrative purposes. Czech at this time was the most developed of the Slavonic languages, and the Bohemian capital, Prague, became first an important seat of European culture and then the centre of a dynamic religious revolution. Lacking an administrative or cultural centre of their own and deprived of political independence for many centuries, the Slovaks easily succumbed – voluntarily – to the attractions offered by adoption of the closely related and comparatively rich Czech literary language. Indeed, even the Hungarian national monarch, Matthias Corvinus, employed it in his royal chancellery.

The Reformation, while it brought momentous changes in many areas, did not shake the hold of Czech, which continued to be used in legal and administrative documents as well as in private correspondence by Catholic and Protestant Slovaks alike. For the first time it appeared in works of literature, chiefly with a religious content. However, it was not written usually in quite the same form as in Bohemia and Moravia, a strong tendency to 'slovakize' being understandable in view of the distance of the Slovak area from the important Czech cultural centres. The trend towards increased slovakizing was soon reversed among Slovak Protestants who, as an outcome of the close ties uniting them with their Czech coreligionists in Bohemia and Moravia, adopted the language of the late-sixteenth-century Kralice Bible for their own liturgy and religious writings and continued to regard it as the sole literary norm until the fifth decade of the nineteenth century. During the long period of its use, and particularly after the suppression of Protestantism in the Czech lands following the lost battle of the White Mountain in 1620, a time during which the Slovak Lutherans helped to preserve the Czech Protestant tradition from total extinction, this Biblical language (*bibličtina*) was transformed into something almost sacred which only profane hands would attempt to alter. It became an obligation to hand it down untouched from generation to generation. Religious exiles from the Czech lands helped native-born Slovaks in this task. But it still proved impossible to exclude the influence of the vernacular on the style of individuals writing for private purposes. Slovak Protestants continued to slovakize when the vigilant eyes of the church press's proofreaders, who were often Czech immigrants, were absent. By the eighteenth century they were doing this almost as markedly as their Catholic fellow countrymen who, having no reason to treat the Czech language with quasi-religious veneration, regarded it merely as a convenient vehicle of expression.

For the Catholic church in north Hungary the Reformation had meant a serious setback. The overwhelming majority of the area's inhabitants had become Protestant, including not only German-speaking townsmen and Slovak-speaking peasants but almost the whole nobility as well. Despite their deeply rooted Hungarian patriotism and in some cases their Magyar origins many Protestant nobles – and some Catholic ones too – became patrons of, and often themselves cultivated, the Slovaks' literary language, Czech. The Catholic Reformation in the seventeenth century changed the situation radically. The Protestants were now reduced to a comparatively small minority.[2] The recatholicized aristocratic families, with a few notable exceptions, no longer took any interest in Slovak culture: they ceased their patronage of the indigenous literature and assimilated more and more to the general cultural pattern of the Hungarian magnate class. The peasantry along with the lesser nobles continued to speak a variety of Slovak dialects but these groups were not at that time culture-producing elements. Only the small Protestant intelligentsia, consisting mainly of clergy, guarded carefully the purity of their people's literary language, Czech.

The setback to Slovak culture that resulted from widespread recatholicization had, however, an unexpected outcome, for it eventually led to the adoption of a truly Slovak vernacular as the language of literature. This development, at least at the beginning, was not the result of any conscious design to replace a foreign by the native tongue. It was not done with any anti-Czech bias: indeed, the same baroque piety prevailed now in the recatholicized Czech lands as among Slovak Catholics. Its source must be sought elsewhere; it stemmed from the efforts of the apostles of the Catholic Reformation to bring their message to the Slovak people, to wean them from the heretical faith that had contaminated them. In order to win them back and to hold them after their reconversion their new spiritual mentors needed to speak to them in a tongue they understood without difficulty. And Czech, it was found, did not fulfil this function adequately, for, though still comprehensible to the educated, it presented serious difficulties to the illiterate or semiliterate masses. The Jesuits were pioneers in developing a Slovak vernacular, followed by other religious orders like the Franciscans and the Camaldolese. At the Jesuit university founded in Trnava in west Slovakia in 1635 a printing press was set up which, beginning in the second half of the seventeenth century and continuing until the university's transference to Buda in 1777, produced a long series of books written in a language in which the norms of literary Czech (now in any case in a state of decay in the Czech lands) were increasingly modified by Slovak elements.

Gradually these clerical authors became conscious of the fact that what they were writing was not really Czech but their native Slovak tongue.[3] Jesuit Slovak (*jezuitská slovenčina*), as it is usually known today, was based on the speech of educated persons in west Slovakia, the most culturally developed part of the country and the centre of Jesuit activity. Slovak linguists sometimes refer to this speech as cultured West Slovak (*kultúrna západoslovenčina*). West Slovak constituted a *koiné*, that is, an amalgam, of several dialects, heavily influenced by Czech, and it was used by Protestants as well as Catholics.[4] The Jesuits, of course, were interested primarily in the upper and educated classes and in defending the faith against Protestant attack. But the movement they had generated was taken further by popular preachers who spoke directly to the masses in their sermons, prayers, and pastoral activities.[5]

By the second half of the eighteenth century the zeal of the religious missionary, though it had by no means entirely disappeared, was being replaced in the aims of the Slovak-speaking Catholic clergy by a desire to educate the people in a spirit compatible with the doctrines of the church. In the age of enlightenment the religious fury of previous centuries was dying down almost everywhere in Europe. In central Europe the reign of Joseph II (1780–90) constituted a watershed in this respect. Religious toleration and the improvement of the peasantry's cultural as well as material conditions were among the foremost aims of his administration. His attempt on grounds of public utility and for purposes of centralization to replace Latin by German as the official language of the Hungarian kingdom evoked strong opposition on the part of the nobles (the *natio hungarica* as they considered themselves) and gave birth to a movement that soon found widespread support among them to put Magyar, only recently being cultivated on a wide scale, in place of either Latin or German as the state language.

Joseph II's policy of imposing German in public life, however, did not exclude his support of the various vernaculars of his realm as necessary for the protection and education of his poorer subjects. He issued a decree to this effect in December 1786. Government officials, he considered, must be able to explain legislation to the various peoples in their own languages, and the clergy (Joseph II looked on the church primarily as an instrument of state policy) could only be effective in civilizing and schooling the raw masses if they mastered the language in everyday use in their parish.[6] Thus, it is not surprising that the first concerted attempt to raise the Slovak vernacular to the rank of a literary language took place during the decade of Joseph II's rule; his support for vernacular education and the folk languages provided an impetus that his promotion of official German did not succeed in offsetting.

The emperor of course was no democrat. A typical product of the Enlightenment, he wished change to come only from above, from the decrees of an absolute monarch. He did not contemplate the overthrow of the existing social order which guaranteed a privileged political position to those of noble rank. In Hungary, as in other parts of central Europe, nobles alone, in theory, made up the nation. And only an ethnic group possessing an indigenous noble class might qualify for nationhood. Thus, in Hungary, alongside the *natio hungarica*, embracing persons of Slovak, Serb, Ruthenian, and Rumanian speech as well as the Magyar-speaking majority, the *natio croatica* was recognized because Croatia possessed a separate administration and its own historical nobility. (The Croats used Latin as their official language as did the Hungarians.) In existing conditions there could be no Slovak nation: those Slovak speakers who enjoyed noble rank belonged to the *natio hungarica*, while the rest, according to official theory, belonged to the *plebs* along with all other non-noble inhabitants of the kingdom, including those whose mother tongue was Magyar.

We have outlined the linguistic developments among the Slovaks that led in the course of the eighteenth century to the emergence in the Catholic community of a literary language, still perhaps Czech, but incorporating broad vernacular elements. Before turning to its conscious elevation into a separate Slovak language during the 1780s, we shall consider briefly whether there existed a parallel trend in the sphere of political ideology to elevate the amorphous Slovak ethnic group to the status of a separate nation, either limited, in the contemporary sense, to the 'feudal' landowning class, or given a more extended, more modern meaning. Only in the latter case could the independent Slovak language introduced by Father Anton Bernolák in the 1780s be viewed as in some measure reflecting an already emerging consciousness of genuine nationhood.[7]

Various attempts have been made from different points of view to show that such consciousness did exist at that date. But a feeling of separate ethnic identity is not necessarily the same as consciousness of separate national identity. Blacks in the United States, for instance, have always been aware that they form a different ethnic group from American whites, but until very recently their leading spokesmen have striven for membership in the American nation on an equality with whites. Though this stand may perhaps foreshadow a black nationalism, its protagonists surely cannot be considered black nationalists, for their aim has been to enter more firmly into, rather than to opt out of, the American national community. A similar situation existed amongst eighteenth-century exponents of Slovak ethnic consciousness until at least the 1790s. This is true, for instance, of the apology drawn up by a Catholic priest, J.B. Magin, in 1723 at the request of the Slovak-speaking nobles of the county of Trenčín to rebut claims that the Slovaks were a conquered people inferior to persons of Magyar origin. It is also true of the literary activities much later in the century of two learned priests, Juraj Papánck and Juraj Sklenár, who drew together a number of themes developed in isolation by earlier writers. Along with attachment to their mother tongue and a vague consciousness of its relationship to the other Slav languages, these writers expressed above all their conviction that Slovak 'ethnics' should enjoy equal status within the *natio hungarica*. They were not even asserting the existence of a separate *natio slovaca* of the nobility, let alone a Slovak nation in the present-day meaning of the term.

However, Papánek in his *Historia gentis Slavae* (1780) and Sklenár in his *Vetustissimus magnae Moraviae situs* (1784) did introduce a concept of considerable importance for the later development of a truly national Slovak ideology: the idea of the Great Moravian state of the ninth century as the creation of the Slovaks (which could easily develop into the concept of Great Moravia as a Slovak national state). After its downfall, Sklenár argued, the Slovaks, who were the country's original inhabitants, entered into a free union with the newly arrived Magyars and fused with them on equal terms. The Slovaks were allotted a civilizing role vis-à-vis the still semibarbaric Magyars: Saint Cyril and Saint Methodius, who brought Christianity to the area, were presented as Slovak culture-heroes rather than as immigrants from the Balkans.[8]

Both Papánek and Sklenár composed their treatises in Latin, the language of learning. The creator of independent Slovak, Father Bernolák, also wrote mainly in Latin. After he became convinced of the need to make a clean break with Czech and employ Slovak where previously Czech or slovakized Czech had been used, Bernolák saw his chief task in giving a firm theoretical basis to the new literary usage, for which only Latin appeared suited. In 1787 he put his views before the public for the first time in two short works: *Dissertatio philologico-critica de literis Slavorum* ... followed shortly by *Linguae slavonicae ... orthographia*.[9]

The writer with the best claim to have launched the use of literary Slovak was not Bernolák himself but another country vicar, named Jozef Ignác Bajza. But Bajza, who 'broke the ice' (as he put it[10]) by writing a two-volume novel of adventure in the Slovak vernacular as early as the first half of the 1780s,[11] was incapable of creating a serviceable literary instrument out of an uncultivated vernacular. He lacked training in philology and his impetuous disposition was disinclined to acquire a sound knowledge of the subject. Moreover, his heavy style narrowed the appeal of his many writings, which included five volumes of sermons covering three thousand pages of print as well as a number of pamphlets in addition to the novel just mentioned. Much of his work he had to publish at his own expense. Bajza's language, which differed less radically from Czech than Bernolák's, was a curious medley based primarily on cultured West Slovak but drawing, too, quite unsystematically on Moravian and Ruthenian dialects as well as on Polish and Croatian (as Bernolák later pointed out[12]).

The motives that led Bajza to innovate are not difficult to discover. In his novel he expressed his concern for the material and cultural well-being of his countrymen. One of the characters, for instance, lamented the fact that the Slovaks, despite their long history, had never had a literature in their own language nor possessed books from which they could easily learn about their land and its past.[13] Despite the serious obstacles facing anyone bold enough to attempt writing in Slovak, with its great diversity of dialects (creating a situation, he said, worse than at the building of the tower of Babel), Bajza declared his unreserved support for his 'mother tongue.' Thus, he wrote in 1787, his fellow Slovaks would 'see that their language too, whatever the initial difficulty, could serve for literary purposes, and ... once they could have their own books, they would not need to rely on foreign ones.'[14]

Bajza was not the only one at this time who felt the need to break with the traditional language in order to spread both enlightenment and religion more effectively among the people. In 1784 there had opened within the precincts of the castle in Bratislava (German: Pressburg; Hungarian: Pozsony) a new educational institution, the Bratislava general seminary, one of a number of similar schools set up by Joseph II throughout his dominions with the object of training young men for the Catholic priesthood in the new enlightened spirit. During the brief period of its existence (it closed, a victim of the anti-Josephinist reaction, after the emperor's death in 1790) the Bratislava general seminary became the matrix of *bernoláčina*, the new literary medium.[15] Bernolák himself studied at the seminary from 1784 to 1787, the year in which he published his first defence of literary Slovak. Encouraged by the emperor's support for training officials, including ecclesiastics, in the various vernaculars and supported by many of their own teachers, the Slovak seminarians had already begun to use the vernacular both in school exercises and in the deliberations of the literary society (Societas excolendae linguae slavicae) which they had set up two years before Joseph II's decree of 1786. They did this, above all, as a preparation for their future role as pastors and educators of the people.[16] In a way the publication of Bernolák's treatises may be considered a collective effort by these Slovak seminarians and their mentors among the faculty.[17] They canvassed likely sympathizers for financial support,[18] and the views expressed by Bernolák probably represented the group's consensus. The fact that in 1787 Bernolák remained anonymous indicates that the young and still inexperienced author regarded his exposition not merely as an expression of his own views but even more as a statement of opinions shared broadly by all his colleagues.

*Bernoláčina*, writes Robert Auty,[19] 'differs from Czech markedly in phonology, but the morphology is drawn essentially from the Czech literary language as codified by earlier grammarians' like Pavel Doležal, whose *Grammatica slavico-bohemica* was published in Bratislava in 1746. 'While the phonology of *bernoláčina* ... does in fact exhibit many of the features of Western Slovak it also shows important elements that tally with Central Slovak usage.' This is probably due to the fact that Bernolák drew heavily on the speech of his native region, Orava, which is essentially a Central Slovak dialect. Although *bernoláčina* contains folk elements like its predecessor, Jesuit Slovak, from which it is not sharply differentiated,[20] its basis is the language of educated persons and not peasants. In his *Orthographia* Bernolák writes that here only the language of cultured people should be accepted as the norm: 'non ... plebis, quam cultorum literatorumque, ac bohemismum minime affectatium,'[21] that is, the *koiné* spoken by educated circles in and around Trnava, the ecclesistical centre of Slovakia. And this attitude was in line with his whole philosophy of enlightening the masses from above: he saw his duty in spreading the culture of the upper classes downward, not, as the Romantics were to conceive their task, in infusing new life into it from below.

In his philological treatises Bernolák displayed pride in the beauties of his native tongue (*lingua slavonica in Hungaria* or *lingua pannonio-slava* was how he usually described it). He believed it was the purest of the Slav languages, and the only one to have remained close to the original speech of the Slavs since it was still uncontaminated by outside accretions. Indeed, in places he seems to fuse the concept of a separate Slovak literary language with that of an *interlingua* common to all Slav peoples (late per innumeros fere populos diffusa, uti in Europa alia nulla) and having a history stretching back to Homer's time.[22] He always denied that his rejection of Czech as the Slovaks' literary language was motivated by anti-Czech feelings,[23] though his strong attachment to the Slovak vernacular undoubtedly stemmed from his deeply ingrained Slovak ethnicity.

Ethnic sentiment, however, was not the only motive leading him and his fellow seminarians to become grammarians and to undertake the publication of works expounding the rules of 'correct speaking and writing' in Slovak. The goal of their endeavours, as they clearly state, was the publication of a vernacular translation of the Bible, which would supply Slovak clergy with an invaluable aid in their pastoral work and crown previous efforts to raise the material and spiritual level of the folk culture. For this – ut sic tandem Scripturae divinae vero genuino et native idiomate slavico pro pannoniis Slavis reddi possint – the arduous work of linguistic codification was an essential prelude. Without first establishing the grammatical rules of the language and a correct orthography the task would have proved impossible.[24] In fact, the obstacles in the way of carrying it out proved greater than had been envisaged and a Bible in *bernoláčina* did not appear until long after Bernolák's death.[25]

The major practical achievement of the Bernolák circle, the founding of a Slovak Learned Society, came fairly early in its development. Even before the closing of the Bratislava general seminary in 1790, which deprived Bernolák and his friends of a valuable base for their activities, they had planned to give these a more secure framework by establishing an organization to publish books, secular as well as religious, in the new literary language. In fact they did not get further than issuing a printed announcement of their intentions before the seminary was shut down. The task was then taken up by one who, though a warm supporter of Bernolák's movement, was older than its leader and had been in charge of a country parish near Trnava since 1780, Juraj Fándly. Fándly chose Trnava as the seat of the new society, which finally opened at the end of 1792 under the patronage of Bernolák himself, partly because it was situated near to his home but even more because of its importance as a Catholic cultural centre.

The Society's life span, however, was short, and while it lingered on a little longer in east Slovakia, around mid-decade it had virtually ceased to function elsewhere. During its brief existence it succeeded in publishing a number of religious books whose printing costs were covered by the members' subscriptions, as well as educational literature intended for popular consumption. But its membership was small, and of the approximately 450 members 75 per cent were Catholic clergy (most of them country vicars). A high illiteracy rate among the peasantry and the poverty in which the overwhelming majority of Slovak-speaking townsmen lived prevented the Society from having a wide impact. In addition, the Society's activities were hampered by the poor state of communication between the various parts of Slovakia divided from each other by high mountain ranges.[26]

The influence of this first Slovak learned society was confined of course to the Catholic section of Slovak society.[27] Fándly was no religious fanatic, and Bernolák too was ready on occasion to collaborate with Protestants, but the Society's chief objective was the printing of Catholic literature and this in itself precluded the possibility of making its work a common effort of the two denominations. Yet the promotion of the Catholic religion was only part, if the major part, of Fándly's endeavour. More than any other of the early disciples of Bernolák, including the master himself, Fándly was concerned with the welfare of the people and with making them worthy representatives of the Slovak ethnic group. In his popular writings he concentrated on those subjects closest to the peasants' interests, such as beekeeping, for example, or popular medicine. He proposed the founding of a school of rural economy for villagers and he planned to write textbooks for it, a scheme that proved abortive. Fándly indeed was 'more democratic'[28] than his colleagues and less confessionally minded in a narrow sense. Under the influence of physiocratic ideas he tended to idealize the life of the farmer; he was himself a peasant's son, whereas Bernolák and most of his coworkers were of gentry origin. And in the ferment of ideas generated by the outbreak of the French Revolution in 1789, Fándly imbibed, even if at second hand and rather faintly, something of its dynamic enthusiasm for the third estate.[29] He remained a Josephinist: indeed he regarded the emperor as a model ruler, shared his hostility to the monastic orders, and admired his church reforms. (This attitude, incidentally, brought down on him the wrath of the repentant Josephinist Bajza, who published in 1789 a furious pamphlet entitled *Anti-Fándli*, broadening his attack to cover Bernolák and his whole school.[30]) Fándly's attitude to the masses, however, was warmer and more intimate than was usual among the supporters of enlightenment from above. Lamenting 'the great uncouthness of our villagers' and the neglect of educated Slovaks who had failed to bring them culture in a language they could understand,[31] he seems here to approach the position to be taken by central and east European nationalists in succeeding generations, who regarded the folk as the backbone of the nation and preservation of the folk language as the surest defence of national identity.

But evidence is not altogether clear whether Fándly did indeed go beyond the point reached by Bernolák, who was mainly concerned with creating a more effective linguistic tool for confessional and educational objectives, and did assume the fact of a Slovak national community embracing all Slovak speakers – not merely the upper classes – and possessing an autonomous existence apart from the *natio hungarica*. The letters written to Fándly by members of the Slovak Literary Society and later published by him show that, whatever views its secretary might hold on this question, their authors' chief interest lay simply in 'purifying [the new literary] language'[32] and supplying books in it for use in pastoral and educational activities. There is the suggestion, too, of starting up a journal in Slovak.[33] Certainly the letters refer not infrequently to the Slovak 'nation.' But this term, we know, was also used by Bernolák and his predecessors, though in a restricted sense, so that caution is needed in order to avoid anachronism. Fándly himself harked back to the historiographical tradition represented by Papánek when in 1793 he published an abridged edition of the latter's treatise, together with some added material of his own, under the title *Compendiata historia gentis slavae*. In this volume, and generally in his reworking of the Great Moravian and of the Cyril and Methodius motifs,[34] he presented an idealized picture of the Slovak past that was to influence Slovak nationalists of a later generation.

The Bernolák movement[35] gives an impression of incompleteness, of unfulfilled hopes and abortive ambitions. It produced volumes of sermons in abundance and a few mediocre poets who wrote religious verse. *Bernoláčina* was permitted in Catholic primary schools in Slovak-inhabited areas; some textbooks and manuals of popular instruction were published in this connection. But several decades elapsed from the launching of Bernolák's literary Slovak before a major writer emerged in the person of Ján Hollý: even so, Father Hollý, for all his genius, remained an isolated figure in his remote country parsonage. He had no equals and very few imitators.

Although among the supporters of *bernoláčina* there were several highly placed church dignitaries, including an archbishop of Esztergom, Cardinal Alexander Rudnay, and his friend the influential Canon Palkovič,[36] the movement was confined mainly to modest village priests whose flocks were for the most part illiterate serfs. The hierarchy, with some honourable exceptions, was at best indifferent; sometimes it was actually hostile, as happened in Fándly's case since his views brought him under suspicion of liberalism. The Catholic church of Hungary, dominated as it then was by wealthy magnates and having a Magyar-speaking majority, was not a suitable incubator for a movement seeking to stress the separate identity of a predominately peasant ethnic group. Moreover, as has often been pointed out, *bernoláčina* itself, as a distillation of the language spoken in west Slovakia and fairly remote from the speech of central and east Slovakia, was inadequate for the main purpose for which it had been devised, to provide a unified literary language for the Slovaks of all regions. It remained to the end what it had been at the beginning, a product of the seminary,[37] rather than becoming an integral part of popular culture. Even within the ranks of the Slovak-speaking clergy it did not gain unchallenged acceptance: there were always some Catholic priests who preferred to go on using Czech, if slovakized, to employing the new literary medium.[38] *Bernoláčina* failed, of course, to gain adherents among the Slovak Protestant intelligentsia who, as we shall see, long regarded it contemptuously as a peasant jargon unbecoming persons with any pretentions to refinement.

The movement continued in not too healthy an intellectual condition until the 1820s and 1830s when an enterprising young Slovak lawyer and official in the Viceregal Council in Buda, Martin Hamuljak, together with a few associates in the capital, almost all laymen, endeavoured to instil fresh vigour into it. In 1834 they succeeded in forming a small but fairly flourishing literary association, Unio cultorum linguae et literaturae slavicae Pestanobudensium, and planned first to set up a chair of Slavonic studies at the University of Pest and then to found a newspaper in Slovak. For lack of support and because of official opposition – and also on account of their living at some distance from the main body of their potential supporters – both ventures fell through, and Hamuljak and his associates were forced to content themselves with an annual literary almanac, *Zora*, which appeared irregularly between 1835 and 1840.[39]

Like the poet Hollý, with whom they were in close touch, members of Hamuljak's circle had been strongly influenced by the new nationalist ideology represented by the 'Czechoslovak' poet Jan Kollár, who was then pastor of the Slovak Lutheran congregation in the Hungarian capital. They even chose him as the first chairman of their association, despite his being a Protestant and at that period of his career a supporter of Czech, though a slovakized Czech. After the appearance in the early 1840s of a Protestant version of literary Slovak, which was introduced and supported by young intellectuals led by L'udovít Štúr, a few young Catholic clergymen also adhered to *štúrovčina*. But the overwhelming majority of Catholics, among them Hamuljak, for the time being held aloof (as did many Protestants at first, including Kollár) until in 1851 the Catholics at last reached a compromise with Štúr and his followers.[40] *Bernoláčina* vanished altogether, while from the other side the use of *bibličtina* among the Protestants dwindled rapidly, although it lingered on as the liturgical language in certain conservative congregations until after the first world war.

Before turning to the role of the Protestant community at the beginning of the Slovak national awakening we should pause briefly to discuss what has been well called 'une des plus grandes énigmes qui touchent à Bernolák.'[41] In the preface to his massive six-volume Slovak dictionary *Slowár slowenskí česko-lat'-insko-ňemecko-uherskí*, begun in 1787 and finally published posthumously only in 1825–7, there appears a passage that has given rise to endless speculation. It cites as one of the chief reasons for compiling the dictionary the increased ease with which Slovaks would now be able to acquire fluency in the Hungarian language, knowledge of which the Diet in 1792 had made compulsory for obtaining public office. Thus, it went on, since the Slovaks form the most numerous people after the Magyars, the Magyar language would soon spread throughout the country.

Some writers have doubted whether the passage is authentic, claiming it was inserted by the editor, Canon Palkovič, probably as a sop to rising Magyar chauvinism. Others, such as Daniel Rapant,[42] have maintained Bernolák's authorship, arguing that no real evidence exists to doubt this and that the passage is not in fact inconsistent with Bernolák's general position (even though he may also have wished by means of it to make his work more attractive to Slovaks who had come under the spell of Magyar culture). It is true that the discovery of an earlier version of the preface, written in 1796,[43] indicates that someone, presumably Palkovič, may indeed have tampered in a few places with Bernolák's wording to ward off possible objections from militant Magyar nationalists. But such changes, if a hand other than Bernolák's made them, appear to be of minor importance and not of a nature to alter the essential meaning of the passage.

Bernolák, we have seen, never posited the existence of a *natio slovaca*: his prime allegiance went to the *natio hungarica* of the nobility and its *patria*, Hungary. He was certainly a supporter of equal rights and complete respect for the different vernaculars spoken within the kingdom: his whole career witnessed to his devotion to the cultivation of his Slovak mother tongue and to his interest in the past of his native ethnic group. But he never denied the obligation incumbent on a multilingual country to select the speech of the majority of the ruling nobility as the state language while preserving the free cultivation of the various vernaculars for all other purposes. For many centuries in Hungary this language had been Latin: opposition to Joseph II's policies led in 1792 to the substitution for it of Magyar, so that at least in a limited sphere, a living tongue replaced a dead one. There was nothing inconsistent in Bernolák's support for this change as expressed in the preface to his dictionary, for in his view Hungary would still remain as much a multilingual land as it had been throughout the centuries of Latin's uncontested sway as the official language of the Hungarian *Ständesstaat*. The adoption of Magyar by the Hungarian ruling class did not signify for him now, any more than did their earlier adoption of Latin, the rejection of the other languages of the kingdom, including Slovak, spoken by the nation of nobles.[44] Bernolák's mistake, we may think, lay in misinterpreting the course of future events, because as time went by the proponents of Magyar linguistic nationalism were to clamour increasingly for the establishment of a unilingual Magyar national state and the elimination of the other languages in all areas of public life. Bernolák's Hungarian patriotism had therefore become something of an anachronism by the beginning of the nineteenth century, but it would also be anachronistic for us to think of it as ever having led him to advocate the restriction of Slovak except at the higher levels of state administration.

His contribution to the emergence of Slovak nationalism, and that of the movement he initiated, did not lie in first enunciating the concept of a Slovak nation as an autonomous cultural entity. What Bernolák and his colleagues achieved was something different: their creation of *bernoláčina* paved the way for the eventual acceptance of a Slovak rather than a Czechoslovak interpretation of this concept when it did emerge.

The hold of *bibličtina* on the Protestant Slovaks continued throughout the period when Bernolák, who died in 1813, and his early disciples were active. A few Protestant intellectuals took a not unsympathetic stand towards the new literary language,[45] but most remained negative in their reactions (as on the whole did the Czech intelligentsia – Catholic as well as Protestant). Jiří Ribay, a Slovak Protestant pastor who also acted as the great Czech grammarian Josef Dobrovský's informant on Slovak affairs, was probably expressing the opinion of most of his Protestant fellow countrymen when he branded the Catholics' linguistic usage as 'gibberish' and predicted its new literary form would enjoy only a short life.[46] Nevertheless, even Ribay had to admit that Slovaks found it 'extremely difficult and tedious' to acquire certain Czech usages (such as the letter *ř* in place of *r*).[47]

In the eighteenth century the Slovak Protestant intellectual, in the words of an outstanding representative of that class, Matěj Bél, was 'lingua Slavus, natione

Hungarus, eruditione Germanus.'[48] As with the Catholics the Protestant intelligentsia combined Hungarian patriotism with attachment to the native Slav tongue. We may add to this, especially after Joseph II's introduction of a wider measure of religious toleration, genuine devotion to the Habsburg dynasty: the Protestant intellectuals, like Bernolák and his circle, were ardent Josephinists and even more *kaisertreu* than their Catholic counterparts.[49]

Like the Catholics, Slovak Protestants also found difficulty at this time in distinguishing exactly between the terms 'Slovak' and 'Slav.' These semantic difficulties were complicated in the case of the Protestants by their firm adherence to Czech, in the form of *bibličtina*. The Czechoslovak connection was long thought of primarily as a linguistic one: it had originated indeed in the religious tie established between Slovak and Czech Protestants at the time of the Reformation. Eventually the idea of ethnic unity crept in, so that while for Catholics a sense of community was usually confined to the Slovaks of Hungary, Protestants came increasingly to feel a common ethnic identity binding Slovaks and Czechs together. In both confessions, however, and particularly among Protestants, ambiguity remained: it is impossible sometimes to be sure whether a writer is referring exclusively to Slovaks, to Czechs and Slovaks, or even to Slavs as a whole. Slovak Protestants, when they refer to 'the Slovak language,' usually mean Czech, for this was their literary medium. But when they speak of 'the Slovak nation' they mean solely the Slovak ethnic group in Hungary.[50] It was from the third element in Bél's epigram, the background of German higher education and German learning possessed by many Slovak Protestant clerics,[51] that the impulse was eventually to come for transforming the older and more amorphous idea of the ethnic group into that of the national community. This community was at first conceived in a Czechoslovak, and only later in a strictly Slovak, shape.

Ethnic consciousness within a framework of Hungarian patriotism was the usual pattern among the Protestant intelligentsia as it was with the Catholics. Whereas with the latter *bernoláčina* now formed the linguistic component in their ethnic consciousness, the Protestants looked to *bibličtina* to perform this function. In fact the two linguistic usages were not too far apart: 'the one a form of Slovak inclining towards Czech, the other a form of Czech inclining towards Slovak.'[52] In practice, however much they might despise *bernoláčina* as coarse and vulgar,[53] even the most rigid upholders of biblical Czech slovakized. Sometimes they did so inadvertently, but not infrequently with conscious intent to make their writings more comprehensible to their readers or to help out where the biblical tongue, which was essentially Czech as it had crystallized some two centuries earlier, failed to express adequately modern ways of thought. Even when they observed Czech grammatical forms they tended from time to time to follow vernacular speech in vocabulary and orthography. They combined this slovakizing with a dislike of the innovations, including numerous neologisms, then being introduced into the language by Czech writers centred in Prague like Josef Jungmann. Conservative opposition to modernization, however, was not the only factor at work here: the new Czech presented even more difficulties for the average Slovak than did the archaic Biblical language which at least was familiar to all Protestant Slovaks from its use in the church services.

Around the turn of the century the Slovak Protestants seem to have been less vigorous than their Catholic counterparts in attempting to give an institutional framework to their cultural life. Perhaps as traditionalists they felt less need for this than Bernolák and his circle who had changed the cultural pattern of their denomination. However, the founding by the Catholics of the Slovak Learned Society in 1792 acted as a stimulus, and next year a group of Protestant pastors, led by Dobrovský's friend Jiří Ribay, put forward a scheme for establishing a society for the cultivation of literature in *bibličtina* (*lingua slavica*) and the study of Slovak antiquities. It was to have its own printing press and journal as well as a library. Ribay drew up a prospectus, *Projectum instituti seu societatis slavo-bohemicae inter Slavas in Hungaria*, from which clearly emerges the Czechoslovak orientation then current among the Slovak Protestant intelligentsia.[54]

The project remained on paper. But a decade later a more modest plan was successfully carried out, again largely due to Ribay's efforts, when in 1803 an institute was set up at the Protestant *gymnasium* in Bratislava for the study of Czech language and literature, the Institutum slavicum Posoniense. Jiří Palkovič was appointed to the chair attached to the institute.[55] The choice was not altogether a fortunate one, for the professor proved to be an uninspiring teacher and his occupancy of the chair for nearly half a century prevented its founders' hopes of making it a focus of 'Czechoslovak' culture from being realized. Yet in other ways Palkovič's contribution was extremely important – as publisher, author, translator, and journalist. Indeed, his activities in these fields seriously interfered with his pedagogical duties,[56] so that his students seem to have been torn between irritation at his neglect of them and admiration for his undoubted merits in advancing Slovak culture. In justice to Palkovič we may add that the pittance he received from his chair would have forced him in any event to seek additional remuneration elsewhere.

Protestant endeavours to institutionalize their culture and to keep up with the Catholics in this respect continued during the early years of the new century. The most successful of the several learned or literary societies active about that time was the Erudita societas Kishonthensis.[57] It was founded in 1808 and functioned in southeast Slovakia, its membership drawn largely from Lutheran pastors. Latin was the language of the Society's official proceedings, but its journal, *Solennia*, printed articles in Czech, German, and Magyar as well. Voices were raised pleading for use of the mother tongue of the majority of members[58] (this was considered to be Czech). But on the whole the Society, like other similar associations, did not take an official stand in the matter. 'Members of the Society, at least the older ones ... were in regard to the language question genuine men of the enlightenment, truly tolerant; any kind of linguistic nationalism was completely foreign to them.'[59] Typical in this regard was the scholar Ján Feješ, who helped to start the Society and continued to lead it until his death in 1823.[60] Certainly his supranational Hungarian patriotism led him to oppose forced magyarization and to step forward in defence of the Slovak language when its traditional rights were threatened. (Slovak probably could not have been his native tongue since his mother sprang from a prominent Magyar noble family.) He regarded all the vernaculars of the kingdom as of equal status, including Magyar, and considered that Latin should be retained as the official language of the *patria*, at least until the still distant time when education would have prepared the country willingly to accept the replacement of living Magyar for the dead tongue in the life of the state.[61]

In the Protestant camp the first person of any note to reach beyond the traditional concept of the Slovak ethnic group and introduce, however tentatively, the new idea of a cultural-linguistic nation seems to have been Jiří Palkovič.[62] 'A nation without its own indigenous language' he wrote in 1812[63] 'is no nation properly speaking: having lost its language ... it has also lost its nationality.' However, Palkovič was a lifelong believer in Czechoslovak cultural unity and his nation is always a Czechoslovak nation – when it is not something even broader, for Palkovič, like so many other Slovaks of that time, found it hard to distinguish between 'Slovak,' 'Czechoslovak,' and 'Slav.'[64]

The first step in the emergence of a Slovak national consciousness had been taken by members of the Catholic intelligentsia. They postulated the separate identity of the Slovak language vis-à-vis Czech: Father Bernolák, we have seen, worked out the principles on which this new literary language should function. But Bernolák and his followers (with the possible exception of Fándly) stopped short of enunciating the idea of a modern cultural and linguistic nation. They still thought of Hungary as their *natio*, just as the nobles of the kingdom, regardless of ethnic background, as well as the small non-noble intelligentsia which was largely dependent on them, had done for centuries. Their cultivation of their mother tongue derived from a multicultural concept of the *natio hungarica*. In this respect there was no essential difference between the Protestant and Catholic intelligentsias,[65] except that in the course of the eighteenth century the Protestants had begun to define their ethnic group as Czechoslovak, whereas the Catholics continued to define their identity within the boundaries of Hungary. This divergence became wider after the Catholics adopted *bernoláčina*, leaving *bibličtina* as the sole preserve of the Protestants. But both camps remained unsure of the exact limits between their ethnic group and the Slavs as a whole.

The leap from ethnic consciousness to national consciousness (described below) was to be carried out by members of the Protestant intelligentsia, at first in a Czechoslovak direction and finally, in the mid-1840s, as an assertion of separate Slovak identity. Jiří Palkovič may perhaps be considered as a precursor of this trend. The idea of cultural and linguistic nationalism had arisen in Germany towards the end of the eighteenth century, in large part as a result of the eighteenth-century Enlightenment and the French Revolution, with German nationalism at first taking a rather less political form than in France. From Germany it was carried to Slovakia and other parts of eastern Europe. Whereas the Slovak Protestants had rejected the linguistic 'separatism' of Bernolák and his school, also indirectly the outcome of the eighteenth-century Enlightenment, many of them welcomed the new gospel of nationalism they encountered during their studies at German universities and in their reading in later years. Perhaps the seed then sown would not have produced the crop it did if one particular factor had been absent from the domestic scene. This factor was the mounting wave of Magyar nationalism[66] which challenged the old 'feudal' multicultural concept of Hungarian patriotism. It seemed to force the country's ethnic groups, including the Slovaks, to choose between eventual assimilation to Magyar culture and assertion of their own separate nationhood, at least in language and culture. For good or ill the old Hungary was disappearing. The question remained open whether the new Hungary would become a multinational commonwealth or a unicultural Magyar national state.

# 2
# Slovak nationalism
# and the Czechoslovak idea

We have seen how the Catholic intelligentsia among the Slovaks began to abandon Czech and to develop the principles of Slovak as a literary language in the latter part of the eighteenth century. They were the first to experience a sense of Slovak ethnic consciousness. Although the Slovak Protestant intelligentsia had felt an emotional attachment to the Czech language ever since Protestantism's suppression in the Czech lands after 1620, they began also to absorb German ideas of linguistic and cultural nationalism during the first quarter of the nineteenth century. Even at that time, however, the rising ethnic consciousness of the Catholic Slovaks and the emerging linguistic nationalism of the Protestant Slovaks (the latter for many decades longer to find expression within a Czechoslovak framework) remained confined to comparatively small sections of the intelligentsia.[1] Most educated Slovaks of both denominations continued to adhere to an old-fashioned Hungarian patriotism that found place merely for the cultivation of the Slovak language when this did not conflict with the superior demands of the country's official language – Latin until 1792, Magyar thereafter. This attitude was the rule, especially in the case of the Slovak-speaking minor gentry (the middle and upper gentry were by now mostly magyarized). And as for the Slovak peasants and the artisans who formed the bulk of the Slovak-speaking town population, they possessed scarcely any national or even ethnic consciousness that went beyond an elemental love of their mother tongue, usually the only language they could speak.[2]

Paradoxically, the leap from Slovak ethnicity to Slovak nationalism came about as a result of changed ways of thought in men who at first would scarcely admit a separate Slovak ethnic identity. They regarded Czechs and Slovaks as forming a single unit: this idea of course had been common coin among Slovak Protestant intellectuals for at least a century. And there was a second paradox in the way this leap was accomplished, for the two men who during the 1820s and the 1830s did most to prepare the way for it, the poet Jan Kollár and to a lesser degree the scholar Pavel Josef Šafařík, denied the existence not merely of Czech and Slovak nations but even of a 'Czechoslovak' nation. For them the nation was the Slav nation, comprising the totality of Slav peoples and possessing its own *interlingua*. At least that was their theory. Kollár elaborated a plan for cultural interchange between the various Slav peoples in order to bring the day nearer when Slav unity would become a reality. He published this scheme in 1837 in German under the title *Concerning Literary Reciprocity*.[3] However, Kollár was ready to admit the existence within the Slav totality of what he called 'tribes (*Stämme*)' each with its corresponding 'dialect (*Mundart*).' In fact he posited four subdivisions: Russian, Polish, Illyrian, and Czechoslovak.

Kollár and Šafařík throughout their lives spoke of themselves as Slovaks. Both men were educated in Slovakia in schools belonging to their Protestant denomination before departing for further studies at a German university. Thereafter both spent most of their active careers outside that country: it was indeed difficult in those days for talented young men to find a suitable niche in a comparatively backward region like Slovakia. Kollár for some thirty years was pastor of the Slovak Lutheran congregation in Pest, while Šafařík worked first as director of the *gymnasium* at the Serb cultural centre of Novi Sad and then from 1832 on in Prague. Their absence for long periods from their native region caused them eventually to lose touch with developments there, especially among the younger generation. But before that happened they had profoundly affected the intellectual development of Slovak nationalism.

Their influence expressed itself in two ways. First, and perhaps ultimately the most seminal, was the introduction of a new dimension into the Slovaks' speculations on their identity. For this development Kollár was most responsible. Secondly, there was the campaign, engaged in for a time by Šafařík as well as by Kollár, to 'slovakize' literary Czech so that it could become a truly Czechoslovak language with the contribution of both partners on an equal footing.

In his idea of nationality, writes Locher, Kollár 'borrowed the framework of his thought and his strivings from German philosophy and the German national movement.'[4] He was profoundly affected by the writings of Herder and Arndt and his participation in the huge demonstration by Germany's nationally minded youth at the Wartburg castle in 1817 on the tercentenary of Luther's famous declaration. In 1817 Kollár had just begun his studies at the University of Jena. He was to bring back from them something more than an academic degree. He brought a new idea: cultural and linguistic nationalism. Of course it was not altogether new to the Slovak intelligentsia. Kollár's former teacher at the *lycée* in Bratislava Jiří Palkovič – also an alumnus of the University of Jena – had already identified nation with language in the German fashion; the one, he thought, could not exist without the other. What Kollár did in applying the idea to the Slavs was to proclaim it with prophetic force and with a poet's vision. Thousands read his works. They were to become the common property of the Catholic as well as the Protestant Slovak intelligentsia; indeed they were read in all Slav countries and admired by their educated elites and they alarmed equally both German and Magyar opponents of 'the Slavonic idea.'

It was no accident that the greatest exponent of Panslav ideology was a Slovak.[5] It was no coincidence, either, that Kollár was an ardent supporter of Czechoslovak unity, a viewpoint he derived from the tradition of his church. His doctrine 'was not a reaction against Magyar nationalism, which played little or no part in his early experience.'[6] What was important in Kollár's ideology for the development of Slovak nationalism, however, was not the fact that in theory he acknowledged only one – the Slav – nation[7] or that the national unit whose existence he recognized as a practical reality was Czechoslovak. The point is that his idea of the nation was one entirely divorced from the state and completely dependent on language.[8] 'I have two fatherlands,' he wrote, 'Czechia (*Čechy*) and Hungary. In the latter dwells my body, in the former my spirit.'[9] While Slavdom might provide Kollár with inspiration for poetic outbursts, it was Czechia, the 'Czechoslovak' land, that was always the object of his deepest affection. Hungary remained merely the recipient of his formal loyalty. He had separated *natio* from *patria* and, unlike Slovak intellectuals of an earlier generation, no longer felt devotion to the *natio hungarica*, a 'nation' composed exclusively of the ruling elite in the Hungarian state. Kollár's nation could only be the community of those who spoke the same tongue as he did. It had nothing to do with the political state, nor was it confined within territorial boundaries. Its defences were not laws and historical documents but the right of every human being to give his highest loyalty to the group with which he had the closest ties of the heart. The state was artificial, framed by men for their own convenience: the nation was organic, a natural creation designed by God himself for man to fulfil his highest aims. 'In the nations' Kollár wrote, echoing Herder, 'we come to perceive what humanity is.'[10]

Since language was at the centre of the new national idea, Kollár, together with Šafařík with whom he had been in close contact since 1819, devoted considerable attention to linguistic problems. While regarding the emergence of a common Slav language as their goal, both men rejected attempts to create an artificial Slav *interlingua* that was not organically connected with the evolution of the constituent Slav tongues.[11] 'Czechoslovak' was the medium of literary expression they recognized in practice, along with the various other 'dialects' spoken by the Slav nations (or 'tribes' in their terminology).

They were especially fascinated with the problem posed by the Slovak vernaculars and their relationship to the literary language used by the Protestants of Slovakia. Just as on the Catholic side heightened ethnic consciousness during the eighteenth century and the defence of Slovak 'nationality' had resulted in part from a desire to assert full equality within the *natio hungarica* for its Slovak-speaking members, so now Kollár and Šafařík began to assert the equality of Slovaks within the community of Czechoslovak speakers. They pleaded insistently for a Slovak linguistic presence within the common literary language until the 1840s when events made them unrelenting opponents of the trend towards further linguistic separation. Both men 'slovakized' in their published writings as well as in their private correspondence.[12] But while Šafařík was interested primarily in the contribution to be made by Slovak folk speech in creating a genuinely Czechoslovak literary language, Kollár only too frequently resorted to neologisms to accomplish this end, and his writing therefore had a rather repellent artificiality.[13]

The two men strove for a language that would be both 'a Slovak Czech and a Czech Slovak (chceme slovenskou češtinu a českou slovenštinu).'[14] They believed the Slovak vernacular to be more melodious than Czech, more aesthetically pleasing. Kollár therefore asked: 'When the Slovaks have been willing to sacrifice everything to the Czechs with respect to the [literary] language, why then could not the Czechs give way at least a little bit to the Slovaks?'[15] The correspondence of Šafařík and Kollár reveals their constant feeling of irritation at the refusal of most Czech intellectuals to acknowledge the justice of their claims for allowing Slovak to influence the evolving literary language. Both men recognized the inadequacy of the archaic *biblíčtina* to act as the instrument of modern literature. It could not reflect the needs of contemporary life. But both clung passionately to the Czech connection: perhaps it was just their devotion to the concept of Czechoslovak unity that made it difficult for the two Slovaks to comprehend why so many Czechs rejected their call for reciprocity.

In fact both Kollár and Šafařík soon came to admit a greater measure of Slovak separateness than did most of the leaders of the Czech national revival. Occasionally Kollár seemed to bestow on the Slovaks the status of a separate 'tribe,' a term he usually used only in reference to the 'Czechoslovaks,' and even referred to them as a separate nation, a term he applied in theory only to the Slavs as a whole.[16] In Kollár's view, however, the multiplicity of dialects within Slovakia made it virtually impossible ever to contemplate the existence of an independent literary language acceptable to all its inhabitants of Slav background (this was to become a favourite weapon in the armoury of the 'Czechoslovaks'). In addition,

Slovaks possessed in the Czech language as it had come down to them in the form of *bibličtina* a treasury they should not surrender lightly. Let them build on its foundation and not risk everything in an attempt to raise a raw country vernacular to the level of literature. In comparison with Czech literary culture, Slovak had hitherto been but a sickly plant. Moreover, the creation of yet another linguistic subdivision within the Slavonic family would do irreparable harm to it and weaken its culture still further at a time when it was threatened on many sides.[17] But, however important, these were considerations more of expediency than of principle and did not alter the fact that Slovaks were not Czechs. They were brothers, in fact almost identical twins, but each possessed his own individuality. In numbers, too, Slovaks almost equalled Czechs, and their speech, according to Kollár, was less contaminated by foreign words than contemporary Czech, which was full of 'Germanisms.' And if each respected the positive elements of the other's speech and was prepared to pool resources a modern Czechoslovak culture could emerge as a reality capable of strengthening the cultural heritage of the entire Slav world.[18]

In Buda in 1825 Kollár published a reader, *Čítanka*, in which he set forth the norms he had worked out in conjunction with Šafařík for a Czechoslovak language. His reader was designed for use in the Protestant church schools as well as by adults who wished to familiarize themselves with the language. Kollár regarded the forms employed in his reader as being midway between folk speech and the liturgical language. This was a compromise that he thought could be accepted by advocates of further slovakizing, perhaps eventually even by the supporters of *bernoláčina*, as well as by those who were loath to part altogether with *bibličtina*. In several areas of Slovakia the reader was in fact introduced into the school curriculum, but this happened only where the church leaders of the district favoured Kollár's use of Roman type in place of the black-letter traditional for all publications in *bibličtina*. Indeed, the degree of opposition he now encountered alarmed Kollár temporarily, and for several years he was more circumspect in pressing the adoption of the principles set out in his reader.[19]

A more detailed exposition of the concept of a separate Slovak identity within the Czechoslovak totality, especially in its linguistic and literary aspects, was provided by Šafařík in 1826. Šafařík was Kollár's superior intellectually and was soon to become one of the leading luminaries of Slavonic scholarship. As a student in Jena he had called for printing texts of Slovak folk songs 'exactly as we speak.'[20] But this certainly did not mean he supported the use of the vernacular in works claiming to be literature.[21] Later he told Kollár[22] 'We should look more to ourselves than to the Czechs ... I don't want to be understood, though, as demanding that the language of our people be introduced directly into books. For while I know well a nation can be enlightened, and aroused to a higher life, only in its own language, I consider nevertheless that it would merely damage us still further if we entered upon Bernolák's path.' And in 1823 we find him writing 'as a Slovak': 'Our literature surely is merely a branch of Czech literature; it must be the most ardent wish of us all ... that it always remains so.'[23]

Yet in his pioneer history of the Slavonic languages and literatures, published in 1826, he put aside all his previous doubts and vacillation and came out plainly for the separate status not only of the Slovak language (he used the terms *Sprache* and *Mundart*) but also of the Slovak 'tribe,' which he placed on an equality with the other constituent members of the Slav family, Czechs, Sorbs, Poles, Slovenes, Croats, Serbs, and Russians. A special chapter of the book was devoted to 'the language and literature of the Slovaks.'[24] 'Slovak' he wrote 'forms a separate tongue, even though for centuries in regard to literature the Slovaks for very good reasons have joined in with the Czechs.' The nearest Slavonic tongue to Czech, Slovak was not identical with it; its purest form was the dialect of the central region, which varied more from Czech or Polish than did its western or eastern dialects respectively. (The last point was to be seized upon eagerly by the young Protestants in the 1840s who, under the leadership of L'udovít Štúr, chose central Slovak as the basis for their new literary language.) While disapproving in principle of Bernolák and his school's employment of the vernacular in literature, Šafařík praised their enthusiastic promotion of Slovak culture and expressed a hope that they could eventually be won over to literary Czechoslovak, which would then become the common heritage of Slovaks of both denominations and thus of the whole nation, including all strata of the population.[25] He confided to a Russian correspondent his fears that there was serious danger of 'the Slovak branch and its language' vanishing altogether if an end were not made to the literary schism.[26]

In his history Šafařík presented 'Czechoslovak' not so much as a fusion on equal terms of Czech and Slovak, which was Kollár's notion, but rather as a form of Czech adapted to the needs of its Slovak speakers. The basic grammatical rules of literary Czech would remain unaltered: its vocabulary, however, should undergo extensive slovakizing. 'The nature of the Slovak vernacular (*Landesmundart*) must be taken into consideration by the incorporation of indigenous words, phrases and turns of speech to the extent needed for preserving in its style a genuine Slovak colouring.' Only in this way could both 'the needs of the Slovak people' and 'the mutual literary intercourse between Czechs and Slovaks' be preserved without sacrificing the interests of the less powerful of the two partners.[27]

The reaction aroused in Prague by such proposals was mainly negative. Among the Czech awakeners of that date both Jungmann and Palacký expressed their strong dissent from Šafařík's position, which they regarded as falling not far short of linguistic separatism. On the Slovak side there was a mounting sense of alienation on account of the increasing modernization of Czech carried out by writers in Prague, whose language differed from Slovak even more than did *biblíčtina*. As Šafařík wrote: 'The style common to Czech writers at present can never become the national style of us Slovaks.' Unless the style of Slovak writers drew nearer to popular speech, then like the Hindu Brahmins writing in Sanskrit they would fail to create a truly national literature. It was 'a sin,' he told Palacký (who had gone to school at the Bratislava *lycée*), to continue to regard Czech and Slovak as identical from the linguistic point of view. 'Indeed you Czechs have never listened to a Slovak' speaking his native mountain dialect. Finally, Šafařík appealed to the opinion reached in his later years by abbé Dobrovský, who Šafařík knew carried great authority with the Czech intelligentsia, in support of his own view that Slovak speech should enjoy independent status alongside Czech.[28] Kollár added his voice to Šafařík's, pleading with Palacký in particular for greater consideration of Slovak needs and interests on the part of Czech intellectuals.[29]

These controversies led to a temporary cooling of relations between Kollár and Šafařík on the one hand and their Czech friends in Prague on the other. At the same time the two Slovaks' contacts with leading exponents of *bernoláčina*, dating back to the early 1820s, increased correspondingly in warmth and frequency. Kollár even attributed the Bernolák movement's existence to the Czechs' 'unfairness' and 'lack of consideration' towards the legitimate Slovak claim to linguistic equality with them.[30] His response to *bernoláčina* was a mixture of admiration and distrust. He rejoiced that it enabled the Catholic clergy to cultivate their Slav mother tongue and to encourage its use among their flock. In this respect, he thought, Catholic priests were more active than Protestant pastors. But Kollár was pained by the thought that it divided his people into two conflicting camps and shut them off from the invigorating influence of Czech culture; and he remained extremely sceptical about its future since he doubted whether the Slovaks on their own could provide sufficient support for a flourishing cultural life. Despite his respect for the poet Hollý, whom in the expanded edition of his *Slávy dcera* (1832) he placed in the Slavonic paradise along with the other great Slav poets, Kollár continued to view *bernoláčina* as somewhat uncouth and scarcely worthy of literature. He hoped that 'the middle way between "high" Czech and "low" Slovak,' which he and Šafařík were attempting to follow now by taking whatever was good in Czech and combining it with the positive elements in Slovak, could serve to reunite the Catholic branch of the nation with 'the common Czecho-Slovak trunk' from which it had become detached some forty years before.[31]

In the 1820s and 1830s the centre of the Bernolák movement shifted to Buda and the circle which gathered there around Martin Hamuljak, who was working as a government official in the capital.[32] Hamuljak and his friends were to prove no more willing to give up *bernoláčina* altogether than were Kollár, Šafařík, and their associates to renounce totally the time-honoured Czech connection. But both sides at this time were sincerely interested in achieving a reunion, albeit each on its own terms. Indeed they now had a great deal in common. We have seen that Kollár and his friends, unlike their predecessors in the Protestant camp, no longer stood inflexibly on the basis of *bibličtina* but were themselves anxious to draw extensively on folk vocabulary for literary use – provided that the foundations of Czech grammar and orthography[33] were preserved. Hamuljak, from his side, acknowledged that Czech and Slovak were extremely close and that Slovaks must collaborate with Czechs if they wished to counteract the growing attraction exerted by Magyar culture on their youth. Without such co-operation the position of the Slovak language, largely neglected by educated Slovaks and left to depend for its continued existence on a poverty-stricken serf peasantry, would indeed become desperate. Hamuljak therefore proposed a compromise. Protestants as well as Catholics, when writing for 'the common people,' would use *bernoláčina*, which could be modified to a limited extent by including Czech and other Slovak dialectal elements along with its original west Slovak core. But in publications intended for an educated clientèle Czech might be used by authors who wished to do so, and Protestants would retain the use of *bibličtina* in their churches. All educated Slovaks, he agreed, could read Czech without too much difficulty. The ultimate aim was the creation of a unified Slav literary language.[34]

Hamuljak was indeed a slavophil in Kollár's style. He and his friends accepted the Kollárian, that is, the cultural-linguistic, view of nationality: Hamuljak read and admired Herder.[35] Alarm caused by rising Magyar nationalism helped to bring the two wings of the Slovak national movement together. Moreover, Hamuljak and his circle no longer adhered to the old-fashioned Hungarian patriotism of Bernolák's generation. Adopting Kollár's national idea, they pushed it further than the master was prepared to go; whereas he was never ready to break completely with Czechoslovak unity, they postulated a Slovak linguistic nation.

In the 1830s Šafařík, whose position was perhaps even nearer to Hamuljak's than Kollár's had been, was the first to beat a retreat. In 1832 he moved to Prague, where he came under the direct influence of the leading Czech awakeners. His growing dependence on them for his daily bread led to his rapidly abandoning the defence of the separate status of the Slovak language. Moreover, his long sojourn in Serb-speaking territory had caused him to lose fluency in his native tongue, and he spoke it now only with considerable difficulty.[36] In his great work on Slav antiquities, published in 1837, Slovaks were bracketed with Moravians and Czechs under the common heading 'Czechoslovak section' of the Slavonic peoples.[37] His volume on Slavonic ethnography (1842) treated the work of

Slovak authors who wrote in Czech as an integral part of Czech literature, while 'Hungarian Slovak' was reckoned as merely one of the two divisions of the Czech language (the other consisting of the Czech dialects of Bohemia, Moravia, and Silesia).[38]

Kollár's evolution towards the Czech position was slower than Šafařík's. It was not until the mid-1830s that his *rapprochement* with Hamuljak and the Catholics reached its climax. In 1836 he advised a young Protestant friend who favoured a larger measure of slovakizing: 'Write as your conscience prompts you [provided only that you retain the Czech orthography] ... Whatever is sound will win out in the end.'[39] He continued to blame the Czechs for their lack of understanding; by their intransigence, he complained, they were irritating not only the Slovaks but the Moravians as well. What they were requiring of the Slovaks was not literary reciprocity but 'self-annihilation and unconditional Czechization.'[40]

With Kollár's support a young Slovak pastor, Michal Godra, worked out a compromise orthography designed to win approval from writers of both Slovak denominations and published it in the organ of Hamuljak's group.[41] Godra also made similar suggestions with regard to grammar and syntax. 'The followers of Bernolák must leave out something from their form,' Godra wrote to a Protestant friend, 'and we shall leave out something from our Czech form.'[42] Godra believed that *bernoláčina*, though unsatisfactory, was closer than modern Czech to the average Slovak and that every effort should therefore be made to find a *via media* acceptable to both branches of the Slovak people.[43]

Godra's proposals do not seem to have aroused much enthusiasm outside the rather narrow circle Hamuljak had gathered together in the Hungarian capital. They were indeed premature. But Godra's scheme indicated that on the Protestant side, if there was reluctance to abandon a literary language common to Czechs as well as Slovaks, 'written Czech had ceased to be regarded as an obligatory standard.'[44] At the same time the most alert elements of the Catholic intelligentsia had shown their readiness, if not to renounce *bernoláčina* totally, at least to accept the hand extended from the other side and work towards ultimate unity.

Nevertheless, Kollár's general position was challenged by many prominent Slovak Protestant intellectuals, even by some who approved a moderate degree of slovakizing. There were those, like the aging Professor Jiří Palkovič (whose pupil Kollár had once been), who stood inflexibly on the basis of *bibličtina* and defended it against exponents of a modernized Czech[45] and against those of a more decisive presence of Slovak vernacular within the language. Palkovič called for all to return 'to the classical orthography of the [Czech] Brethren, [which is] the only correct one.'[46] Literary conservatives, however, were not the only ones to look askance at Kollár's attempt to create a Czechoslovak language. For instance, Karol Kuzmány, editor of *Hronka*, in whose columns Kollár published an abridged version of his treatise on literary reciprocity, considered that Kollár had moved too far away from the Czechs in his effort to find common ground with the followers of Bernolák and had thereby endangered that 'union with the Czechs of Bohemia and Moravia' which was essential for the successful development of Slovak literature.[47] On the other hand, when a Czech writer, J.K. Chmelenský, launched a violent attack on Kollár in 1837, Kuzmány, although a supporter at that time of the modernized Czech being written in Prague, rallied to his defence. 'We Slovaks' he wrote 'don't have the ř, and yet for the sake of reciprocity we put up with this; why then can't the Czechs allow our *tá* (*haec*), *tú* (*illam*), *tý* (*illos*), *tj* (*illi*). Indeed this possesses great convenience from the grammatical point of view.'[48]

The younger generation, however, seldom felt the reservations their elders often entertained about Kollár's theories concerning nation and language. From the early 1830s at all the Protestant *lycées* of north Hungary, Slovak-speaking students became ardent adherents of Kollár's 'Slavonic idea.' They accepted his identification of nation with language as well as his belief in the possibility of a joint Czechoslovak literature, though at first many of them continued to regard the latter as, from the linguistic point of view, essentially a Czech literature. Politically they differed from him to a certain extent. While he remained largely indifferent to social problems and increasingly sought support in the Habsburg dynasty for Slovak endeavours, they began to concern themselves with such matters as popular education and the material condition of the peasantry and espoused a very mild form of political radicalism. This they had acquired chiefly through contacts with the Polish conspiratorial movement in Galicia and with Czech student liberals centred in Vienna.[49] But there is no evidence that the Young Slovaks ever went far along the road to revolution. They were in favour of political and social progress but by means of gradual change.[50] They believed that as sons of a peasant people they must promote the welfare of the lower ranks of society and that social change was called for if their nation was to achieve equality with its neighbours. With all of them the nationalist impulse predominated and it provides the key to understanding their attitude to politics. But romantic attachment to Slovakia vied in their loyalties with devotion to the all-Slav community, which sometimes became confused in their minds with Russia, the home of the biggest and the only free Slav people. 'One heart, one blood, one tongue ... and one fatherland' was their motto.[51] 'First Slovaks, then Czechoslavs but also Slavs too' was how their priorities usually ran.[52] Eventually they were propelled by their nationalism into an alliance with the reactionary forces in Vienna.

At the Bratislava *lycée* a Slovak student society (Společnost česko-slovanská) had come into being in 1828,[53] and in the 1830s similar groups were formed in several other Protestant *lycées*.[54] These groups kept in touch with each other and with the Bratislava society which was the most flourishing one. After a few years of comparative inactivity it had begun to blossom under the guidance of L'udovít Štúr. Štúr, who reached the age of twenty in 1835, was a born leader. Eloquent, industrious, with the power to inspire unbounded devotion in his peers – and sometimes in his elders too – he possessed a fine mind as well as unlimited energy. It was Štúr, along with Michal Hodža and Jozef Hurban, his fellow students in Bratislava, who in the next decade would take the final step in the creation of literary Slovak and in making the Slovaks a modern nation.

The professed purpose of all these student societies was cultivation of 'the mother tongue,' by which was meant the Czech language, though they often called it 'Czechoslav.'[55] As future pastors and teachers (almost the only careers open to them) the members needed practice in *bibličtina*. Some of them were interested, too, in experimenting with the vernacular. Since they needed books to accomplish their aims, they collected libraries.[56] In their leisure time the students explored the Slovak countryside together, climbed some of the Tatra mountain peaks, or organized festivities with speeches and songs in praise of the Slovak people. The best known of these gatherings took place on 24 April 1836 when Štúr and his friends met in the ruins of the medieval castle at Devín, once a centre of the Great Moravian state. Here they solemnly assumed Slav names: Štúr became Velislav, Hurban Miloslav, and so on.[57]

At the Bratislava *lycée* the German students had had a society since 1788 and the Magyars theirs since 1790. None of these societies, including the Slovak one, succeeded in enlisting the support of more than a small fraction of the total number of students of the school, and even in the senior classes members in each society constituted a minority of their respective language group. Much the same pattern prevailed in other *lycées*. Everywhere one of the chief aims of the Slovak societies was to win the allegiance of the new students whose national consciousness was often as yet uncrystallized. Uncertain concerning their nationality, or sometimes unwilling at first to commit themselves definitively, they gravitated most easily towards the Magyar side since this represented the dominant culture in the state.[58] German culture too, though on the decline in north Hungary, still exercised a strong hold on the towns of the area, and it was in the towns that these Protestant schools were located.

Almost at once the Slovaks faced a knotty problem. They had formed associations in order to deepen their knowledge of their native tongue. But what was this language? As we have just seen, they usually referred to it as Czech or Czechoslav or occasionally Czechoslovak. The different names reflected their uncertainty concerning its precise shape. They were confronted with several alternatives. Should they follow the example of Professor Jiří Palkovič, holder of the

Bratislava *lycée*'s chair of Czechoslovak studies, and cleave to the traditional *bib-ličtina* while supplementing its deficiencies in modern vocabulary by a somewhat surreptitious incorporation of Slovak dialect? Should they abandon it as hopelessly archaic and join with Prague intellectuals in using a modernized Czech, despite this being geared to Bohemian rather than Slovak needs? Should they instead adopt Kollár's position wholeheartedly and strive for the creation of a truly Czechoslovak language, even at the expense of increased friction with Czech writers in Bohemia? Or should they not rather press on towards winning a victory for the vernacular as the Slovaks' literary language, even if mainly for use in the more popular branches of literature?

Adoption of *bernoláčina* was not considered by the Young Slovaks as a serious possibility. They admired Hollý's poetry[59] and sought contacts both with Hamuljak's circle and with young Catholic seminarians, and they ardently desired eventual literary reunion with Bernolák's followers. In particular they appreciated the fact that *bernoláčina*, for all its faults, was far closer to the hearts of the majority of the Slovak people than was Czech, and much more easily comprehended by them.[60] But, like Kollár, they envisaged this reunion only on the basis of Czech, as modified to be acceptable to the other side.

Because of the strong impact of Kollár's works on the Young Slovaks most of them at first accepted his arguments in favour of a Czechoslovak literary language. Also popular among them was Šafařík's view, expressed in 1826 in his history of the Slavonic languages and literatures, that at least vernacular Slovak should be classed separately from Czech. Hodža, for instance, voiced this opinion in a paper read to the Bratislava society in September 1833. It did not, of course, prevent his simultaneous support of the term 'Czechoslav' for Slovak literary production. In justification he pointed to the degree of 'refinement' reached by the Czech language in comparison to the crudity of Slovak, which also remained hopelessly fragmented into dialects and subdialects without any standard form. What was needed, he thought, was neither Czech vernacular nor Slovak vernacular but an extract of both prepared by men of letters drawn from the two constituent parts of the nation.[61]

In the 1830s Štúr, too, supported the Kollárian position and attempted to guide his friends along the same path. On the one hand he felt ill at ease with 'new Czech'; on the other, he experienced difficulty at first in observing the rules of 'the classical Czech preserved in Slovakia by Jiří Palkovič and others,' though he attempted to keep to them except when recording folk songs.[62] 'We're indeed in purgatory' he complained.[63] If they wrote in Czech the ordinary people, especially the Catholic majority, could not understand them; but if they wrote in something nearer 'to our own language (*k nářečí našemu*),' then they would cut themselves off from the Czechs. This, in his opinion, would be a disaster. Nevertheless, the Czechs should make concessions to the Slovaks in both grammar and vocabulary. 'Then a Czechoslovak language (*řeč*) would emerge in fact and not merely in name.'

It was extremely difficult for Štúr and his friends to find a way out of their dilemma. They resented Czech attempts to impose linguistic innovations on them that had not grown organically out of the Slovak soil. But *bibličtina*, it was clear, could not serve much longer as a serviceable instrument for developing a modern culture, though it might have to be kept for use in the church where its premature removal could only cause unnecessary upheaval. As for Czechoslovak in the style of Kollár, they began to experience doubts here too. In view of the strongly negative reaction it had evoked among Czech men of letters and on account of a growing consciousness of its essentially artificial character, they began to wonder whether a Czechoslovak language of this kind could ever become a reality. Štúr in particular was extremely sceptical.

In their writings the Young Slovaks continued to 'slovakize,' to the distress of the editors of the only two Slovak literary journals existing at that time, *Tatranka*, which Palkovič tried to maintain as a model of 'classical' Czech, and *Hronka*, where Kuzmány made 'new' Czech the rule.[64] From the point of view of men like Palkovič and Kuzmány the worst example was set by young Samo Chalupka. Chalupka is claimed, with some justification, as the first in Štúr's group to write a literary work in modern Slovak.[65] But it is clear that Chalupka at this stage never envisaged abandoning Czech as the Slovak literary language or jettisoning the concept of a joint Czechoslovak literature.[66] Kollár and Šafařík remained heroes to him as well as to most of his colleagues, including Štúr himself. What many Young Slovaks were calling for with increasing insistence during the late 1830s and early 1840s, though not unanimously or without frequent vacillation, was the use of the vernacular in publications intended for circulation among peasants and artisans, whose knowledge of Czech was very limited. 'Why should I be bothered with that Czech?' was apparently the reaction of many ordinary people.[67] Among well educated persons, the Young Slovaks still believed, Czech usually presented no insuperable obstacle to understanding the printed word.

The whole issue was debated by the Bratislava students at innumerable meetings. When the question arose of starting a journal of their own, Chalupka took the lead in pressing for the use of 'a more Slovak Czech' in its columns. For lack of money, however, the project had to be abandoned.[68] Until the schism of the mid-forties, in fact, a Czech periodical, *Květy*, almost from its first appearance in 1834 continued to act as mouthpiece for the Young Slovaks. Both *Tatranka* and *Hronka* appeared only irregularly, and the latter, for lack of funds, ceased publication altogether in 1838. Not only did *Květy* publish their articles but it reported sympathetically and in detail on the cultural life of Slovakia. Yet neither the liberal attitude of the paper's editors nor the anxiety of its Slovak contributors to make full use of its columns prevented friction over the language question, which increased as the Slovaks became more and more sensitive to Czech attempts to moderate or even eliminate their slovakizing altogether. In 1841 we find Hurban protesting indignantly to the chief editor, Jaroslav Pospíšil, a Czech, in the name of all his colleagues against editorial tampering with their manuscripts. The editor should not forget that they were 'by no means Czechs.'[69]

It was only a short step from there to an open declaration of linguistic independence. In 1839 Hurban had written: 'Since we are one family, rightfully and with justice [Slovaks] demand that a Czech poet be not only a Czech but a Czechoslav.'[70] But appeals of this sort found little response in Prague, and this indifference and the neglect of Slovak interests on the part of the Czechs discredited the idea of Czechoslovak cultural unity, in which the Young Slovaks had at first put so much trust. Kollár's repeated advice to them to stand inflexibly behind the Czechoslovak idea, not only on their own account but for the common good of all Slavdom,[71] began to wear a bit thin. The belief grew stronger that, contrary to Kollár's opinion, the Slovaks did indeed constitute a separate Slavonic nation (or 'tribe'), separate, that is, from the Czechs. Every nation should possess its own language (the Young Slovaks did not part company with Kollár here): this principle gave Štúr and his friends yet another argument in favour of elevating the vernacular to independent status. Other influences leading towards the eventual literary break (*rozkol*) with the Czechs, such as the political situation inside Hungary, made it seem advisable to try to solve Slovak problems within a strictly Hungarian framework.[72]

The idea of a Slovak nation and language, which became the battle-cry of the *štúrovci* from early 1843 onwards, appeared to be incompatible with further maintenance of the Czechoslovak idea. The literary offspring of Kollár, the Young Slovaks, had now repudiated his work. For several years, however, no open rupture occurred between Štúr's group and Kollár and his followers. Part of the reason for this lay in the fact that they were active partners in the bitter struggle waged within the Lutheran church of Hungary between the Slovaks and the Magyar liberals, which began with the installation in September 1840 of a Magyar liberal nobleman from north Hungary, Count Károly Zay, in the office of general superintendent.[73] Among several issues in dispute between the two parties language rights figured most prominently. Therefore Kollár and Štúr worked together in support of the petition presented in Vienna on 4 June 1842 by Slovak Lutherans in defence of the position their culture had traditionally enjoyed in the old multilingual Hungary, a position now threatened by the growing movement to create a unilingual Magyar national state.

By the end of the 1830s Kollár had followed in Šafařík's footsteps and, rein-
ing his slovakizing impulses, had finally made his peace with the literary pundits
of Prague. Jungmann wrote on learning that Kollár had 'come back to pure
Czech': 'I have joy over him more than over ninety and nine just persons.'[74] Even
so, Kollár continued to be sensitive to slights from the Czech side. Why did the
*Matice česká* continue to neglect Slovak writers like Jiří Palkovič who had devoted their whole lives to the pursuit of a common literature? he asked a friend
in Prague in 1844. 'But to what purpose such regrets and grievances?' With the
début of *štúrovčina* the previous year, Slovaks now used three instead of two
literary languages. Kollár believed this was due above all to Czech indifference to
the Slovaks' justified complaints and to their disdain of Slovak efforts to create
their own literary tradition. 'Today I stand almost alone in my love for unity
and reciprocity, and I fear I may be the last Slovak who writes in Czech and
maintains Czecho-Slovak concord.'[75]

Kollár, however, did not remain inactive for very long in face of the threat to
the Czechoslovak idea posed by Štúr's decision to use central Slovak for *belles-
lettres* and the enthusiastic reception this got from many young Protestant intellectuals. Kollár began to rally support for the traditional Protestant position with
the intention, as he put it, of 'making an end to this nonsense and fanaticism.'[76]
Backed by Šafařík he proposed to the Bohemian Museum's Committee for Czech
Language and Literature in February 1846 that they publish a volume of articles
attacking *štúrovčina*. Kollár in Pest was mainly responsible for gathering the contributions. He acted quickly and the book came out in Prague in May of the same
year under the title *Voices concerning the Need for a Unified Literary Language
for Czechs, Moravians, and Slovaks.*[77] Its appearance brought about a decisive
break within the Slovak national movement between the older generation of
Czechoslovaks and the younger Slovaks who followed Štúr's lead.

It cannot be said that the 'voices' heard in Kollár's volume had anything particularly new to say. Some of the materials had been printed before, such as the
contributions from Jungmann and Palacký and from the Slovak poet the late
Bohuslav Tablic. Of the original articles the most interesting perhaps was from
Šafařík, who wrote as 'a Slovak born.' Šafařík still held that Slovak dialect, if
firmly enclosed within the Czech grammatical and orthographical matrix, had a
modest place in Slovak writings intended for popular consumption. But this did
not alter the fact that in his view there was a single literary language common to
Czechs, Moravians, and Slovaks to be employed in works composed for an educated public. Štúr's action now signified a complete break with the past; to cut
the old links between Slovakia and the Czech lands in this fashion was to weaken,
perhaps irreparably, the position of the former, the less robust of the two partners.[78] For his part Kollár, unlike Šafařík, was often rude, sometimes almost in-

sulting, in the way he spoke of his opponents. He claimed widespread support in Slovakia for retaining the Czech literary connection – not with entire justification, as events were to show – and argued that Štúr represented only a handful of bookish and inexperienced enthusiasts.[79]

While the Czech contributors, as well as Šafařík,[80] wrote in favour of the new, modernized Czech, the Slovak contributors, most of whom were country parsons or village schoolteachers, were obviously thinking of *bibličtina* – 'our beautiful, pure, biblical Slovak' as one of them called it[81] – when they spoke out against Štúr. In many cases they regarded the old biblical language as a protection against the Czechization of the language threatening from Prague. Thus Kollár, the former literary innovator, now headed a conservative reaction, and in the realignment taking place within the Slovak Protestant intelligentsia all that was young and intellectually alive tended to gravitate towards Štúr's camp. Henceforward, aging expatriates like Šafařík or Kollár himself, church dignitaries like Jan Seberini, ecclesiastical superintendent of the mining district of central Slovakia, and a host of highly respected but elderly Lutheran clergymen formed the backbone of the Czechoslovak 'party.'

At first Kollár's offensive against Štúr and his followers seemed fairly successful. The clergy in Seberini's church district, assembled in their annual conference in Pest in August 1846, even went so far as to call for a boycott of publications printed in *štúrovčina*, urging all pastors and teachers publicly to condemn its use.[82] However, the appearance of Kollár's *Voices* does not seem to have aroused the interest in Slovakia that its sponsor had hoped for.[83] Several other writers stepped forward to defend the Czechoslovak idea, including two of Kollár's associates, Štěpan Launer[84] and O.H. Lanštják. Both of them were considerably younger than Kollár. In the early 1840s Lanštják had been a student at the *lycée* in Levoča, where he wrote romantic verse filled with slavophil and patriotically Slovak sentiments,[85] and Launer a student at the Bratislava *lycée*. But Launer, who then taught at the *lycée* in Banská Štiavnica, spoilt his case by abusive and scurrilous attacks on Štúr; and both he and Lanštják offended many potential sympathizers by their lukewarmness towards Slovak claims to nationhood. In 1848 both men supported the Magyar national cause.[86]

The Czechoslovak idea did not disappear altogether from the Slovak scene after 1848. In the 1850s under Vienna's patronage *bibličtina*, in the form of so-called Old Slovak, regained its former ascendancy, but only temporarily. Štúr's group, which had come under a cloud during the clampdown of the Bach regime, and the young Catholic intellectuals, some of whom had flirted for a time with Old Slovak, soon agreed to pool their resources and adopt a slightly modified *štúrovčina. Bernoláčina* now vanished, while *bibličtina* continued to be used for some time in a dwindling number of Protestant churches. But the need to maintain close ties with the Czechs was never forgotten, despite periods of friction and the recurrence of mutual recrimination. The emergence of a Czechoslovak state in 1918 and its reinstitution in 1945 reflected the vitality of the Czechoslovak idea. But first from the Slovak side and finally on the part of most Czechs came a realization that the political association essential for the survival of both peoples could only grow out of mutual recognition of their separate identities. This involved recognition of a Slovak nation with its own language and literature and the right to develop a culture different from that of the Czechs.

The Slovak 'Czechoslovaks' of the first half of the nineteenth century contributed to the development of Slovak national consciousness almost as effectively, if not as directly, as Bernolák and his associates had done a little earlier.[87] They brought back from their studies at the Protestant universities of Germany the notion of the modern cultural and linguistic nation and planted it firmly in Slovak soil. Thereby they provided the small Slovak intelligentsia with an ideology more adapted to the contemporary world than the old-fashioned ethnic group consciousness that had prevailed hitherto among the intellectual elites of both denominations. Secondly, whereas Bernolák's creation of a Slovak literary language served to demarcate more exactly than before the Slovak identity vis-à-vis the Czechs, the Czechoslovaks were the first to disentangle the Slovak nation from the Hungarian state. They did this by rejecting the idea of a *natio hungarica* in which a Slovak ethnic group might participate as an equal partner with the Magyars and the rest; to the Czechoslovaks a nation of this sort seemed a monstrosity because neither historical traditions nor the existence of an independent state but the possession of a language in common made a nation out of a collection of people who lived together.

Bernolák had declared the Slovaks culturally independent of the Czechs while he retained their tie with the old Hungarian idea. Kollár and his associates, though devoutly attached to the Czechoslovak position, which they viewed within a panslav framework, at the same time broke the Slovaks' affiliation to a Hungarian nation. They acknowledged, if somewhat hesitantly, separate Slovak needs within the framework of Czechoslovak cultural unity. Their experiments in slovakizing, which they eventually repudiated, inspired a younger generation to attempt something much bolder, to postulate a separate Slovak nation that would correspond to the separate linguistic identity towards which Kollár and his school had been groping. To do this Štúr and his disciples had to break with the Czechoslovaks. In large measure it was sons against fathers. But *štúrovčina* and the new concept of Slovak nationality did not emerge simply in reaction against the Czechoslovak idea nor as a product of the political circumstances in which the Slovaks then found themselves. They were born out of the Slovak Czechoslovaks' strivings towards nationhood for the Slavs of north Hungary.

# 3
# The making of
# a Slovak nation

During the years immediately preceding the revolutionary upheaval of March 1848 Slovak nationalism underwent a radical transformation.[1] Its contours were redrawn and its design reframed on a new model. The change came from the efforts of a section of the Protestant intelligentsia. These men were mostly young, students of theology or pastors and schoolteachers just out of college. As a result of their work the nationalism of the Protestant intellectual elite changed from being predominantly Czechoslovak in form to specifically Slovak in both form and content.

The Catholic Bernolák and most of his disciples, though breaking the Czech connection, had continued to feel closely linked to their Hungarian fatherland. They defended the Slovaks' right to equality in the *natio hungarica* with the other ethnic groups, including the Magyars. But even if a few of them, like Juraj Fándly, the enlightened Josephinist abbé, ceased to think of the *natio* as exclusively noble in composition, most of Bernolák's disciples, and certainly Bernolák himself, never abandoned their old-style Hungarian patriotism.

The French Revolution had equated the nation with the people; the German Romantics, led by Herder, identified the nation with the language spoken by the people. This new idea of nationality came to exercise an immense influence on the intellectual elites of all the stateless nationalities of east-central and south-eastern Europe. The first to bring the idea to Slovakia had been the young Protestant intellectuals returning from their studies at Jena or Halle, the poet Kollár among them. Not only did Protestant Slovaks eagerly seize upon it but young Catholic intellectuals such as Hamuljak did so too. Kollár, like Hamuljak, lived in Pest; he was therefore able to influence cultural developments in Slovakia only indirectly. In the 1830s Protestant intellectual activities became centred, as we know, at the old Lutheran *lycée* in Bratislava. The dominant figure among Slovak students at the *lycée*, Ľudovít Štúr,[2] was a village schoolteacher's son, and therefore a man of the people. More than anyone else Štúr was to be responsible for restructuring the ideology of Slovak nationalism during the half-decade before 1848.

At the very time when Štúr and his friends were completing their studies or just beginning their careers as pastors or teachers, Slovak culture was entering a period of crisis. Towards the end of the 1830s it became clear that a confrontation was imminent between the Slovak Protestant intellectual elite and the representatives of the Magyar liberal nationalist movement. The principles of Magyar nationalism differed fundamentally from those of Slovak nationalism or the nationalisms of a number of other stateless peoples of eastern Europe. It retained the essentially political basis of the old Hungarian 'feudal' patriotism. But at the same time, chiefly as a result of the influence exercised by the emergent nationalisms of west European countries like France, it extended the concept to embrace the whole population living within the borders of the state. Magyar nationalism, therefore, like Western nationalism (and to some extent the contemporary nationalism of the Poles, too), was linked primarily to the state, not to the language. In their endeavour to modernize the state, Magyar nationalists now sought to replace Latin by Magyar as the official language of Hungary. 'This principle,' the Hungarian historian Gogolák observes, 'concealed within itself the source of future conflicts.'

According to Herder and his disciples in eastern Europe the nation was a product of nature with an inborn right to develop its own language and culture, while the state was an artificial phenomenon: to deprive the nation of this right was a crime against humanity. On the other hand, according to Magyar nationalists the state-nation alone possessed the right to call itself a nation and to ask for official protection for its language and culture. In Hungary the Magyars formed the state-nation, the rest were merely 'nationalities' without collective rights beyond those personal rights enjoyed by all citizens of the country.[3] Although the first of a long series of legislative enactments giving Magyar a privileged position beside the still official Latin had been passed by the Hungarian diet as early as 1792, the scope of this legislation was limited and it remained to a large extent inoperative. More serious for the Slovaks was the 'extralegal' action of the county assemblies and other organs of opinion controlled by the nobility.[4] Although these attempts to magyarize were seldom implemented, they indicated the rising support for magyarization on the part of the Hungarian ruling class and its waning belief in the old multicultural Hungarian idea. In justification of such measures Magyar nationalists, the liberals in particular, pointed to the danger of panslavism and to the threat from Tsarist Russia; increasingly, in fact, 'Magyar public opinion failed to distinguish between ... panslavism and ... the Slovak national idea.'[5]

Kollár seems to have been sincere in his repudiation of political ends. His slavophilism aimed at cultural reciprocity among Slavs rather than at their political union. Along with many other Slovaks, including the Catholic poet Ján Hollý, he admired Russia: after all it was then the only independent Slav state, and a big power at that. No conclusive evidence was ever produced in support of Magyar nationalist suspicions that Russian intrigue lay behind the Slovak national movement. In fact this was a chimera, which some Magyar patriots, like the liberally inclined conservative Count István Széchenyi, had the courage to denounce as such.[6] The Slovaks' desire to maintain and develop their language and culture drew on German rather than Russian inspiration. Indeed, the example set by the Magyars themselves undoubtedly stimulated the Slovaks and other peoples of the kingdom to emulate their cultural achievements and even to resist them when they attempted to deny to others what they demanded for themselves.[7] The Magyar nationalist view that Slovaks and the rest constituted merely 'nationalities,' with no claim to cultural autonomy since such rights were the sole prerogative of the Magyar state-nation, naturally failed to convince the Slovaks.[8]

In 1844 the Diet finally replaced Latin by Magyar, now widely known as 'the national language (a nemzeti nyelv),' as the sole vehicle of its proceedings and of the country's administration. Magyar also became – theoretically – the only language of instruction in all schools within the frontiers of Hungary proper (i e excluding Croatia and Transylvania which continued to be considered as separate territorial entities). This legislation marked the climax of a movement that since 1825 had been gaining impetus as Magyar cultural life went through a period of renewal. 1844 symbolized the end of an epoch in Hungarian history.

A few years earlier north Hungary had become the scene of a passionate struggle within the Lutheran church between Magyar liberals and the Slovak party.[9] The latter, though probably voicing the sentiments of the majority of church members, was often outvoted at church assemblies by the influential and extremely vocal Magyar minority. The Slovak leaders represented a predominantly peasant people; the Magyar liberal members included several titled aristocrats and a number of country gentlemen and men of wealth and education. In September 1840 open conflict broke out after Count Károly Zay was chosen general inspector of the Lutheran church in Hungary. Soon after assuming office Zay launched a twofold campaign, first, to make Magyar the official language of the church and its educational institutions and, secondly, to bring about a union with the Hungarian Calvinists. Since these were almost all Magyars and since, moreover, the nationally minded Magyar gentry enjoyed even more influence in the Calvinist than in the Lutheran church, it is not unreasonable to suppose (as the Slovak Lutherans did) that Zay's aims were not purely ecumenical but included a good dose of nationalist politics as well.[10]

Before 1848 the impact of magyarization had fallen most heavily on the Slovaks. The Magyar nobility was well entrenched in their region and had reason to expect opposition only from a small and politically powerless intelligentsia. In addition, the Slovaks possessed neither legally guaranteed political rights like the Croats or Germans nor a church organization entirely separate from the Magyars like the Serbs, Rumanians, and Ruthenians (Ukrainians).[11] A separate church could provide a bulwark against denationalization in an age and in a country where culture and religion were closely interwoven. But the Slovaks, both Catholic and Protestant, belonged to denominations in which the Magyars enjoyed political, and in the case of the Catholics numerical, ascendancy. This made the Slovaks vulnerable to assimilation in areas vital to the preservation of their indigenous culture; in particular it endangered the position of the mother tongue in the elementary school system controlled by the church.

Even his enemies acknowledged Count Zay's personal rectitude,[12] but even some of his friends may at times have wondered at the frankness with which he spoke of his intention to magyarize the Slovak Protestants, 'our Slav brethren.' Of course Zay did not envisage the forcible eradication of their language from private use: policies of this kind have been a twentieth-century refinement. What he aimed at, now that the Diet was making Magyar the language of all branches of government, was to extend its reach still further by imposing it on the Lutheran church, over which he presided. He hoped soon to see it oust *bibličtina* from the liturgy and church administration, and he was determined to make Magyar the language of instruction in the church schools where it would replace *bibličtina* at the elementary and Latin at the higher levels.

Zay justified the need 'to magyarize (*zu magyarisiren*)' his Slovak coreligionists by pointing to the Russian threat and by identifying the Slovak national movement with Russian-inspired panslavism. The Magyars, especially Protestant Magyars, stood for liberty, culture, and progress; Russia and the Slav cause for ignorance and despotism. The choice, he believed, was 'freedom or the knout.' Since Poland's fall 'the Slav speech' had 'ceased to be the language of freedom' and become instead a destructive element. Unless the Slovaks assimilated to Magyardom, Protestantism in Hungary as well as the country's political independence would disappear before the onslaught of the Eastern tyrant: 'Whoever doesn't grasp this will understand nothing.' There should be no hesitation, therefore, in sacrificing 'etymological researches and linguistic exercises,' which in other circumstances might have been entirely harmless, for the sake of 'the common good of mankind,' including the good of Hungary and the Slovaks themselves. All should 'strive vigorously for that great goal of magyarizing the fatherland.'[13]

Zay's colleague, Ferenc Pulszky, who was later to become Lajos Kossuth's close associate during the Hungarian war of independence in 1848-9, was even more frank. The Slovak majority, he wrote, 'are made up of the lowest material of civilization.' The nobility had become Hungarian and the middle class almost entirely German; the Catholic clergy supported magyarization, so that cultivation of a Slav tongue was dependent chiefly on the efforts of 'impecunious Protestant pastors.' 'The Czech language [sic] has no future in Hungary.' He concluded by advising Kollár, its leading advocate, to follow his friend Šafařík's example and remove himself from Hungary to Prague where he would do less harm.[14]

The Slovak Protestant leaders naturally did not greet this invitation to cultural suicide with much enthusiasm. They accused Zay of concealing his designs against them under 'a pretence of liberalism.'[15] Štúr's letters from this period, for instance, are filled with alarm and foreboding about the results of Zay's campaign. Wrote Štúr: 'We believe assuredly that everyone for whom his nation and its culture as well as Protestantism lie near to the heart ... will fight' against the attempt to smother the Slav heritage.[16]

Church union was indeed defeated. The struggle to maintain the traditional position of the Slav tongue within the church was harder and more prolonged. For at least a decade Protestant publicists had been writing books and pamphlets defending this position against encroachments from the side of the Magyar nationalists. The number of such works increased in the early 1840s as the pressure from the Magyar side became stronger.[17] Many of them also restated the Slovak view of nationhood as an expression of separate cultural and linguistic identity, taking issue with the Hungarian view that recognized the full nationhood of state-nations alone.[18] Almost all these works were published in German, which made the Slovak case widely known throughout central Europe (most educated Magyars as well as Czechs and Slovaks knew German well). They were usually published in Leipzig in order to escape the heavy censorship of the Metternich regime. The Hungarian censors, though in general more lenient than their counterparts on the Austrian side, were particularly severe in deleting passages referring to the Slovaks' nationhood.[19] In the absence of a regular Slovak press this pamphlet literature helped to strengthen nationalist feeling in the Slovak Protestant community itself,[20] for there were still many there whose attachment to the idea of Slovak nationhood was less than lukewarm.

At the beginning of the 1840s the Slovak Lutherans, with little hope of gaining more than paper assurances of support and sympathy from outside public opinion and with every expectation of losing the struggle going on inside the church against the socially influential party led by Count Zay, began to consider seeking recourse in Vienna for what they considered the injustice now being done them. Ever since the king-emperor, Joseph II, issued his edict of toleration, Slovak Protestants had displayed warm loyalty to the reigning house. Moreover, there were elements at court strongly hostile to the Magyar nationalists and favourable to the non-Magyar nationalities of Hungary. The Slovaks might even hope for the protection of the most powerful man in the realm, Prince Metternich, and they could be pretty sure of support from his influential rival Count Kolovrat, a Bohemian aristocrat of Czech extraction. Thus emerged the plan to present a petition to the monarch setting out the Slovaks' grievances and the ways and means for putting these right.[21]

Originally it was planned to include Catholics as well as Protestants in the protest. But this idea was abandoned in order to avoid accusations from the Magyars of stirring up panslavist unrest in the country; the whole affair was therefore limited to Protestants.[22] For tactical reasons no attempt was made to obtain signatures on a mass scale: in the end only about two hundred appeared on the document. A number of drafts were drawn up before the final text was agreed upon, several having been composed for submission to the Hungarian Diet rather than to the ruler. The petition, which was presented in Vienna on 6 June 1842 by a delegation of Lutheran clergy, included no hint of territorial autonomy for the Slovaks. Such a proposal had indeed figured in several earlier drafts, the first time the Slovaks had voiced a potentially political, rather than a purely cultural, form of nationalism. But the text now presented asked only for the maintenance of the traditional position of the mother tongue and for protection against further magyarization in their churches and schools. The establishment of a chair of Slavonic languages at the University of Pest was almost the only positive demand made by the petitioners. The petition was essentially defensive, carried out in a conservative spirit and aiming at the preservation of the status quo (as, for example, in the request for continued use of Latin in church records and conference minutes). Though both Kollár and the younger Štúr and his friends had been active behind the scenes, men like the two church superintendents Jozeffy and Seberini (who was to support the Kossuthists in 1848) gave the tone to the document that went to Vienna.

Archduke Ludwig received the delegation on behalf of the emperor and, while generally non-committal, gave its members reason to hope for a positive response from the government. But disillusionment soon ensued. A wild outcry arose from Kossuth and Zay's party and from the whole Magyar liberal press, which accused the Slovak Protestant leaders of treason in taking their case outside the country.[23] A number of enquiries and a second petition to Vienna were needed before the monarch, after consulting the Palatine of Hungary, finally responded in May

1845. Several minor concessions were eventually gained, a lull ensued in attempts to magyarize the Lutheran church and the elementary school system dependent on it, and the projected church union was not realized. But it was clear that the hopes placed in Vienna had not been fulfilled. Salvation for the Slovaks would not come from that quarter. The Slovak Protestant intelligentsia, including the younger generation which felt the disappointment of its hopes more keenly perhaps than older and more experienced leaders, did not abandon altogether its Austroslav orientation (this was to be renewed in 1848-9). But conviction grew that in future the Slovaks must rely chiefly on their own strength, on the resilience of the ordinary people, and that policy should be directed towards strengthening the latter's ability to resist denationalization. This was the most important lesson for them that emerged from the experience in Vienna.[24]

The appeal to Vienna and the need to cultivate good relations at court led Štúr and his young friends for the time being to cast overboard their earlier sympathies for the Polish cause and any thought of clandestine activities. Štúr even defended the Holy Alliance in a tract and described its member states as 'guardians of the peoples' rights.'[25] He had come to associate political liberalism with the policies of the Magyar opposition: Vienna, however reactionary, seemed at least to offer limited cultural freedom to the Slovaks. If liberalism meant Kossuth, then far better Metternich. At the same time, however, resolution of Slovak problems would have to be sought within the framework of Hungary. It seemed unlikely that Slovak culture could be safeguarded any longer through the Czech connection. Was such a connection, in fact, still meaningful in the circumstances of the 1840s? Did a 'Czechoslovak' nation and language really exist at all? The stage was set for a new scenario.

Early in 1843 Štúr and his closest associates at the Bratislava *lycée* (where Štúr, since returning from the University of Halle, had been assisting Professor Palkovič) took a momentous step. They started to use the vernacular, justifying their action with the argument that the Slovaks constituted a nation entirely separate from the Czechs and therefore must write in their native speech.

Štúr's decision reflected what historians in Czechoslovakia have sometimes defined as his *politicum hungaricum*, that is, his reorientation of Slovak cultural politics towards the Hungarian scene. But the decision had deeper roots than this. Mounting disillusionment with Vienna and with 'high' politics, which had failed to produce the expected results, provided the setting in which tendencies long maturing within the young Protestant intelligentsia finally found fulfilment. Hopes of gaining, or rather regaining, the petty nobility of north Hungary for Slovakdom, a factor stressed in particular by writers like Milan Hodža or Albert Pražák,[26] seem to have influenced Štúr and some of his colleagues at this time. These minor nobles still talked Slovak in their daily life. Few of them spoke much Magyar. They clung to Latin, the traditional language of the Hungarian nobility, and even if they had only a smattering of it their ignorance was usually no greater than that of their Magyar-speaking counterparts. Now that the struggle to retain Latin as the language of the noble-dominated county assemblies and of local administration seemed lost for ever, some of these Slovak nobles began to speak up in favour of using the Slovak vernacular. They preferred it to Czech because the latter was unfamiliar to most of them. Towards the end of 1841 two petitions, organized by D'ord' Kossuth[27] (surprisingly, a relative of Lajos Kossuth, whose family came from north Hungary) and signed by 151 other members of the petty nobility of mid-Slovakia, supported Štúr's request to the authorities to publish a newspaper for his countrymen and asked that it be published 'in their own tongue.'[28]

In Hungary, where traditionally only nobles had enjoyed political rights in the state and only state-nations were endowed with the attributes of nationhood, the Slovak national movement had keenly felt the lack of a truly Slovak noble class. The time now appeared ripe for a *rapprochement*. The Slovak nationalists were once again turning their gaze back from Vienna to the Hungarian scene, while the Slovak nobility seemed to be finding its way back from 'Hungarianism' to its Slovak roots. But the apparently favourable circumstances proved deceptive. The older generation of the Slovak-speaking nobility still clung desperately to their antique Hungarian patriotism while the younger nobles were fast losing the last remnants of Slovak sentiment and assimilating to Magyardom.[29] The Slovak nobles, it is true, opposed Kossuth's party, but more because of its political liberalism and its program of social reform than because of its views on the national question. The nobles defended the social privileges of the old ruling class, including its cherished exemption from taxation, whereas the Slovak nationalists needed to frame their program so as to win the peasant masses. Once elected to the Hungarian diet in 1847, Štúr spoke up manfully in favour of peasant emancipation even though his election had been due to backing from the party of the conservative magnates. In the end nothing resulted from the hopes placed in the Slovak-speaking nobility.

Thus we may conclude that Štúr's *politicum hungaricum*, while externally a conservative manifestation, was basically populist and nationalist. First the expectations of Štúr and his friends in the 1830s that radical political action, or at least alliance with central European liberalism, would further the cause of their people seemed to have proved groundless. Then, the attempt to gain Vienna's support for the Slovaks had run into serious difficulties. Though something might still be achieved from that quarter, it would clearly not be what the Slovak Protestants had originally counted upon. Uncertainty arose even about the effects, at least the direct effects, of Slavonic cultural reciprocity. Štúr's generation did not cease to believe in the idea. But they came to realize that Slav unity was a distant goal and the threat to Slovak culture an immediate danger.

Where could the young Protestant intellectuals now turn, except towards their own people? They must speak to them in their own tongue, the speech they used themselves in their most intimate moments and had learnt on their mothers' knees. For some time they had been finding it increasingly irksome to curb the urge to slovakize in their writing and increasingly irritating when Czech men of letters censured them for it. Ordinary folk, it was clear, had even more difficulties on this score. The average Slovak peasant could scarcely be expected to comprehend Czech when even educated Slovaks sometimes experienced difficulty understanding it. Štúr and his friends were agreed that they must help educate the masses, help raise them to a level where a truly national culture could become a reality. This could be achieved only if the vernacular ceased to be a peasant jargon and became a literary language. Of course a price must be paid: the ancient and close connection between Slovaks of the Protestant persuasion and Czechs would have to be sacrificed. To sever this connection would certainly be painful. It was contemplated only because the alternative seemed worse: the ultimate dissolution of the Slav culture of north Hungary in the rising tide of Magyardom. The Štúr group felt the linguistic break was inevitable since the Czechs and their literature could not help the Slovaks out of their present unenviable situation, and it would have its compensations. For one thing, the separation would not be complete because Czechs and Slovaks would remain united at a higher level in the all-Slav community. (Štúr's Young Slovaks continued to be firm believers in the Kollárian panslav concept.) Again, separation from the Czechs would help reunite the severed Slovak cultural community; Protestants as well as Catholics would henceforward write in the mother tongue and the longed for reconciliation between the two intelligentsias could be consummated.

A formal resolution to adopt written Slovak was taken at a closed meeting at the Bratislava *lycée* held 'between three and four in the afternoon' of 14 February 1843.[30] Only Štúr himself and five others were present, but their decision was subsequently approved almost unanimously by the other nationally minded students. Štúr and his friends had been encouraged by news, recently received, of continued support for the vernacular on the part of the minor Slovak nobility. They had been alarmed, and at the same time strengthened in their resolve to opt for the vernacular, by another piece of news – the month before, Vienna had temporarily prohibited the use of the Illyrian name of the movement led by the Croat Ljudevit Gaj. This suggested that Metternich might be unwilling to tolerate Czechoslovakism much longer, because, like Illyrianism, it presented its group as a subdivision of Slavdom.[31] 'The same will happen to Czecho-Slovakism as has just happened to Illyrianism' wrote twenty-one-year-old Ján Francisci, then one of

Štúr's most devoted admirers.[32] Threatened now, it seemed, from Vienna as well as from Buda, yet hopeful of winning the support of the top and bottom strata of Slovak society, the young Slovaks felt the time had come to launch on a course of action they must have been privately considering for months.

How long their linguistic separatism had existed is difficult to say. It had matured gradually. Separatism was not simply a matter of philology; it was also the outcome of a changed outlook on the national question. Štúr and his students at the *lycée*, as well as his two close friends Michal Hodža and Josef Hurban,[33] who were now both installed in country parsonages, seem to have remained 'Czechoslovaks' until 1842, or even the beginning of 1843. Till then we find Štúr doing everything he could to dissuade his young friends from departing too radically from the standards of literary Czech.[34] Yet several years earlier, while Štúr, in Halle, was encountering Hegel's conception of history as the progressive manifestation of Spirit reflected in a succession of peoples, Hurban had already talked of the Slovaks as a separate tribe (*kmen*) from the Czechs, 'tribe' in Kollárian terminology being roughly equivalent to 'nation.' At first Hurban saw the Czechoslovaks forming a duality composed of two equal partners[35] (the same idea Šafařík had held a decade or so earlier). But by the end of 1842 Hurban had altered his tune: 'For a long time we've been at odds with the Czechs,' he wrote, 'we've got to proceed seriously. We're Slovaks through and through; there's nothing Czech about us. Our works are the offspring of a spirit that's thoroughly Slovak, so why don't the Czechs recognize us as being different?'[36]

If we disregard their slovakizing of the literary language, which had been going on for some time, we see that the Young Slovaks' enunciation of tribal, or better national, separateness preceded a declaration of linguistic separatism. The new literary language emerged as a result of their gradual shift in national identification; it did not cause this change of identity. A true nation, they argued, must cultivate its own language. Kollár, Šafařík, and many other good 'Czechoslovaks' had slovakized in their writings, but they continued to adhere to the Czechoslovak idea of nationality and consequently to the Czech language. Štúr and his friends decided to employ the vernacular in place of Czech only after becoming Slovak, instead of Czechoslovak, nationalists.

At first they proceeded cautiously, using Slovak only in their private correspondence and in the minutes of student gatherings at the Bratislava *lycée*. In the summer of 1843 Štúr, Hodža, and Hurban met at the latter's parsonage at Hlboké and reached a further decision; to make new Slovak the medium of literary intercourse for the whole people.[37] Štúr, though, was still feeling his way. At the beginning of the new school year in October he warned the students against attempting to replace *bibličtina* by new Slovak in the curriculum; such a move, he realized, could damage their cause at a time when it was threatened both from inside the Slovak camp and from outside. Besides, a premature step could harm the whole future of Slavonic studies at the *lycée* because Slovak culture was then under strong attack from Zay and his party within the church. Their parents had sent the boys to the *lycée* to learn 'biblical' Czech, and such wishes must be respected. Moreover, Štúr went on, they would need to know Czech in their clerical careers.[38]

Supporters of new Slovak were anxious as well to dispel the idea that their decision stemmed from hostility to the Czechs. 'Don't imagine that it means we want to break away from you,' wrote one of them to a Czech friend. 'Not at all! It has been done because hitherto other Slav nations (*národy*) have not regarded us as a separate *natio* (*kmen samostatný*) possessing in Hungary its own political rights.'[39] It is clear the group, in their precarious position in Hungary, wished to avoid losing Czech support, while at the same time hoping to assuage, or perhaps to counter, Magyar hostility by defining their nationhood within a Hungarian framework.

'Štúr's [new literary] language' writes Robert Auty 'represented a kind of *koiné* of the central Slovak dialects'; it was 'a composite language,' based essentially on the variegated speech of mid-Slovakia but with 'a certain admixture of Western Slovak elements and a strong lexical parallelism with Czech.' No single dialect formed a basis for *šturovčina*. Scholars used to point either to the Liptov dialect or to the dialect of the Zvolen area as its core. Today Slovak linguists regard it as a codification of the speech of educated persons from central Slovakia, and they speak of this as forming a cultured Central Slovak (*kultúrna stredoslovenčina*) parallel to the West Slovak *koiné* that Bernolák in the 1780s had taken as the basis of his new literary language.[40] Whereas Bernolák's disciples were drawn at the outset mainly from west Slovakia, then the most important cultural centre in the country, Štúr's followers came predominantly from the central region.[41] Culturally this region had lagged behind the western area, but it was beginning to catch up. Moreover, its central position made its speech more adaptable for use as a national language than the speech of either the western or eastern regions. This factor, combined with the alienation they felt as Protestants from the culture of the Slovak Catholics, undoubtedly played a role in the Štúr group's steady rejection of *bernoláčina*, in spite of their admiration for the poetry of Father Ján Hollý and friendly contacts with him and many other members of the Catholic intelligentsia.

Once launched, *šturovčina* spread fairly rapidly in the Protestant community, especially among the younger members of the intelligentsia.[42] The conversion to new Slovak of numerous young pastors and village schoolteachers opened the way to its eventual acceptance by the common folk. But this still lay in the future. Many educated persons accustomed to Czech found it difficult now to switch to a different usage, even if they had previously proved unable to write Czech without unconscious slovakizing.[43] Among the leaders of the movement there were continual disputes at this time concerning the precise shape to be given to the new literary language. Hodža, in particular, disagreed with Štúr on many points of grammar and orthography, as well as on the Slovaks' exact position within the Slavonic family,[44] while Štúr had difficulty accepting many of his colleague's rather extraordinary neologisms. For a time these disagreements cooled the warm friendship between the two men.

One work of Štúr's did more than any of his other writings to unite the younger Protestant intellectuals behind him – his treatise, *The Slovak Tongue, or the Necessity of Writing in This Tongue*, which appeared in 1846.[45] An emotionally charged manifesto, it was passionate, poetic, and rhetorical. The arguments are cloudy and repetitious, the terminology frequently imprecise, and the organization poor. But Štúr was not primarily a philologist or a philosopher of history. Though he cultivated many disciplines, he was single-minded, here as in all his other writings, in striving for his goal: 'the creation of a nation,' the reinvigoration of 'Slovak national life.'[46] The very defects of his treatise combined with the author's obvious enthusiasm and earnestness helped to carry the day.

'Slovakia for long has been asleep,' Štúr began, but it is awakening.[47] He went on to explain why it had become necessary to make Slovak a literary language. The main reason for this he saw in the awareness now reached that the Slovaks formed a separate nation or tribe within Slavdom (*národ slovanský*). The very essence of this separateness lay in the Slovaks' possession of their own language, the folk speech, the expression of their innermost being.[48] Štúr praised the Slavs for their highly developed *kmeňovitost'*, a virtually untranslatable word he used to cover two rather different concepts: the proliferation of a large ethnic collectivity like the Slavs into separate nations, each constituting an organism with its own individual richness of culture, and also the spirit that infuses them. The ancient Greeks and the modern Slavs were to him examples of highly developed *kmeňovitost'*, while peoples like the ancient Romans and the modern Magyars,[49] Turks, and Germans lacked this quality. The greater the variety of cultures within an ethnic collectivity, the richer spiritually both the whole and the parts would become.

In contrast to Kollár, who posited only four tribes and languages within Slavdom, Štúr claimed eleven.[50] While he was somewhat ambiguous concerning Bulgarian and Slovene claims to develop a separate literary culture, he had no doubts on this score concerning the Slovaks. 'We Slovaks' he stated 'are a tribe and as a tribe we have our own language which is quite separate from Czech.' No nation could be dependent for its culture upon another whose 'spirit' had grown out of a different historical experience. Czechs and Slovaks must remain very close, as they had been in the past. But the Czech language was no longer easily intelligible to Slovaks, who possessed an ancient, pure, rich, and melodious speech of their own, and, moreover, one that reflected the spirit of their nation, just as the Czech tongue reflected the Czech, but not the Slovak, national spirit.[51] Of all the variants of Slovak, the speech of the Tatra mountain area in the centre of the country (in fact the basis of *šturovčina*) was the one in which this spirit was best preserved. Štúr and Hodža believed that the Tatra region had in protohistoric times been the cradle of the Slav 'race,' and its dialects still occupied a central position amidst the surrounding Slav tongues.[52]

Like earlier Slovak writers referring to their people's past Štúr stressed the priority of Slovak settlement in north Hungary. It predated the arrival of the Magyars in the Danubian plain. Having already established a civilized state of their own, the Great Moravian kingdom, the Slovaks, after it was overthrown by the Magyars, helped to civilize the rude Asiatic newcomers. For centuries they lived with the Magyars in amity, contributing more than their share to the prosperity of the multilingual Hungarian state. Hungary had remained the Slovak fatherland. And especially now that they were beginning to write in the vernacular instead of in a foreign tongue, Czech, Slovaks had every right to consider themselves a properly constituted nation within Hungary and to claim equality with the Magyars and the other cultural and linguistic nations composing the state.[53]

Unfortunately for Štúr, arguments of this kind failed to impress Kollár, Šafařík, or a number of other Slovak 'Czechoslovaks,' or the leaders of the Czech national revival like Havlíček and Palacký.[54] They all regarded the schism as an unfortunate and hopefully brief aberration on the part of a few young hotheads. Concerning Štúr, Palacký wrote in a letter to Kollár: 'What a shame this man went to Halle and got mixed up with Hegelianism. Hence all this muck!'[55] And in 1846 Kollár persuaded the Bohemian Museum to issue a collective work attacking new Slovak in often unmeasured terms.[56] Štúr and his friends were indignant at all this 'infamous babbling' about the Slovak language,[57] but their reactions, at least in public, were on the whole more moderate than those of their elders.[58]

Squabbling over fine linguistic points, which occurred within Štúr's group as well, began to seem sterile to many supporters of new Slovak when unaccompanied by positive action to raise the level of folk culture.[59] After a long struggle with the authorities Štúr had finally got permission to publish a newspaper, the first number of which appeared in Bratislava in August 1845.[60] At first he was still a convinced 'Czechoslovak': the decision to employ new Slovak in the paper instead of Czech appears to have been taken in February 1843, that is, about the time of new Slovak's first adoption by Štúr's circle.[61] Štúr had concealed this decision for some time in order to avoid offending prominent supporters of his project who belonged to the Czechoslovak camp.[62] But once launched, writes a historian of Slovak journalism,[63] the paper 'became the most significant focus for organizing various bodies such as reading clubs, societies for economic improvement, adult schools, savings banks and the extremely important temperance associations.' Other activities of the Slovak nationalists during the years before 1848 included co-operatives, amateur theatre, and various aspects of popular education.[64]

Perhaps the most valuable achievement for the future development of the national movement was the establishment in August 1844 of a society named Tatrín. Its founders included both Štúr, who remained in the background, and Hodža, who was elected chairman. The name Tatrín stressed the symbolic importance of the Tatra mountains of central Slovakia as a symbol of national unity. Its model appears to have been the Matica česká, which had come into existence in 1831. The society's aim was to rally all Slovaks who wished to work actively on the basis of the new literary language for the social and cultural development of their people. 'The field of its activities [is] the whole spiritual life of the nation. Ways and means [include] everything allowed by the country's laws.' Thus ran the minutes of the society's first general meeting.[65] Money, however, was always short, and so was time, for the society ceased to function a few months after the outbreak of revolution in 1848. Early that year the Hungarian Viceregal Council had finally turned down Tatrín's application for official approval, which it had left undecided nearly four years, on the grounds that the society was anti-Magyar. Although it could continue to exist legally as a private association, it was restricted in its activities: it was not allowed to publish its statutes or to make any printed appeals to the public or to establish formal contacts with other cultural organizations within the land.[66] Not surprisingly, therefore, Tatrín failed to realize much of what it had planned to do. In fact, its membership never rose above eighty.[67]

Of its projected publications only five actually appeared in print. Although these included such important works as Štúr's grammar of new Slovak and treatises by Hodža in its defence, the school textbooks and other items of a more popular character were never produced. Financial support was also given to patriotically minded students, the names being drawn from members of both religious denominations, and moral support extended to the temperance campaign carried on jointly in this period by members of the two faiths. This kind of undertaking Slovak nationalists rightly regarded as an effective means of raising the cultural level of the people. Nothing, however, was done to implement the proposal to help improve the deplorably low standards of elementary schools in Slovakia. On the other hand, a great deal of time was expended on, and much heat generated by, discussions on the correct orthography to be employed in the new literary language. No agreement was reached, however, before Tatrín dissolved.[68]

'Tatrín,' wrote a prominent Protestant writer soon after its foundation, 'must be the point of our unification with the Catholics; so that they will be ready to accept our Slovak [language], while Slovak Catholic priests will make the school authorities have their school books written in it and seminarians trained, too, in this language.'[69] And in the summer of the following year a Czech observer, František Zach, reported: 'Štúr's efforts today are more Slovak-oriented than Kollár's: he contemplates a cultural-linguistic unification of Protestant with Catholic Slovaks. Thus reunited the Slovaks expect to be in a stronger position to resist the attacks of Magyarism.'[70]

But once again the plans of Štúr and his circle were realized only on a very limited scale. They maintained friendly contacts with the theological students at the Catholic seminary in Banská Bystrica who supported *bernoláčina*,[71] and they collaborated with Catholic clergy in different forms of social action such as the temperance movement. But it soon became clear that the overwhelming majority of Bernolák's followers, including Hamuljak's group in Buda as well as the poet Hollý, were not yet prepared to renounce Bernolák's linguistic model. Early in 1847 Štúr, in an effort to gain greater participation from the Bernolákites, permitted Catholic contributors to his two journals to use their own orthography.[72] And in August of the same year in the course of Tatrín's fourth annual general meeting, held at Čachtice in the parsonage of its Catholic vicar, important steps were taken towards bringing *štúrovčina* into line with Bernolák's orthography. But still the Catholics held back, even though several prominent Bernolákites had taken part in the Čachtice meeting, including the grammarian Martin Hattala and Bernolák's grandnephew Andrej Radlinský.[73] Membership in Tatrín was almost exclusively confined to Protestants, most of whom were either clergymen or school teachers. As yet only a handful of Catholic priests were ready to declare their allegiance to *štúrovčina*.[74]

The establishment of Tatrín partly compensated for the severe loss experienced by Štúr's movement when at the end of 1843 its leader was dismissed from his post at the Bratislava *lycée*. His dismissal had come after a lengthy investigation of the charges of panslavist agitation brought against him by Count Zay's party within the Lutheran church. Štúr's removal in fact signified the end of the *lycée*'s Slavonic Institute as a vigorous centre of Slovak culture, though it lingered on into the third quarter of the century.[75]

In March 1844 twenty-two of the most active and responsible of Štúr's followers among the students left Bratislava as a demonstration of solidarity with their teacher. Thirteen of the twenty-two transferred to the Protestant *lycée* in Levoča which then became a centre of the movement for several years. Štúr himself remained in Bratislava. From 1845 on he was busy editing his *Slovak National News*, and in 1847 he was elected to the Hungarian Diet for the town of Zvolen.

The émigrés spread Štúr's gospel in eastern Slovakia, where Štúr's influence had until then been felt less than in the central and western regions. It remained largely a youth movement, with some of the junior Protestant clergy joining in. A Union of Slovak Youth was set up in Levoča in February 1845 which soon had branches in the other Protestant *lycées* of north Hungary.[76] Its members collaborated with Tatrín and supported the spread of *štúrovčina* and the new national idea, and they participated actively in the temperance movement in the belief that drink was one of the main obstacles to a strong popular culture among the Slovak peasantry. Moreover, unlike Štúr himself who had become increasingly conservative, some of the Union's supporters began to advance radical political views akin to those held in the late 1830s by the Young Slovaks at the Bratislava *lycée*.[77]

The radicals were led by Štúr's former lieutenant, Ján Francisci, who was ably supported by a fiery young poet, Janko Kráľ'. Both men in this period favoured the cause of the Kossuthist liberals – except on the national question.[78] And, unlike Štúr, Hodža, or Hurban, they were hostile to the Slovak-speaking petty nobility whom they considered a retrogressive element in society. It was the peasantry they hoped to arouse to an awareness of social as well as national oppression, though they made little headway towards this goal. In 1847 Francisci, who was now practising law in Prešov, penned a passionate manifesto urging the enserfed peasants to rise up and destroy their oppressors if they attempted to oppose emancipation. He foolishly confided his manuscript, however, to a Polish acquaintance posing as an emissary of the émigré Polish Democratic Society, with whose radical social program Francisci sympathized. In fact the man proved to be an Austrian police agent, and the manuscript disappeared into the archives of the Ministry of Interior in Vienna.[79]

Several fairly productive years on the part of Štúr and his associates were ended prematurely by the events of 1848.[80] These events introduced fresh divisions among the Slovaks and showed that national consciousness was still confined almost exclusively to a small intelligentsia split along confessional lines. The Slovak-speaking masses were largely indifferent to nationalist slogans and appeals. Nor were the intellectuals united. Štúr and his friends called for Slovak autonomy, first within Hungary and later as a separate crown land of the Habsburg monarchy, which brought them into armed collision with the forces of the Hungarian state directed by Kossuth. Others, like the respected Lutheran church leader Seberini, chose the Magyar side as the cause of liberty. Many Catholics remained unengaged.

The struggle against the Magyars aligned the Štúrites, with the movements of the other 'nationalities' of Hungary, on the side of the Habsburg crown, and it brought them back once more to a pro-Czech position. Without Czech support their cause seemed hopeless. Štúr's Czechophilism in 1848, like his Austroslavism, was temporary and based on expediency.[81] But his colleague Hurban's sympathy for the Czechoslovak idea went deeper and was to return after the *Ausgleich* of 1867 when the Slovaks finally lost Vienna's protection against magyarization.[82] During the 1850s the Czech language – in a slightly slovakized form known as Old Slovak – was patronized in Slovakia by the authorities; it won some temporary support, too, in the Catholic as well as in the Protestant camp, mainly it would seem for opportunistic reasons. But Štúr, whose activities in 1848–9 had brought him Vienna's disfavour (he remained under a cloud until his death in 1856), firmly opposed Old Slovak, as did several prominent Bernolákites. In October 1851, at a meeting held in Bratislava, Štúrites and Bernolákites finally reached agreement on the basis of a modified version of Štúr's new Slovak.[83] Next year the Catholic Hattala, who with Hodža had been chiefly responsible for the compromise, published a concise grammar of 'revised Slovak (*opravená slovenčina*),' which spread fairly rapidly among the Slovak intelligentsia from the 1860s on and forms the basis of present-day Slovak.

The making of a Slovak cultural-linguistic nation was now accomplished – in theory. The first step had been taken in the 1780s when the Catholic Bernolák and his circle began to write in the vernacular: this had established a separate Slovak identity vis-à-vis the Czechs. Next, the Protestant Kollár and his friends of the Czechoslovak persuasion in the 1830s and 1840s had redefined the Slovak's position vis-à-vis the Magyars when they ceased to pay homage to the old idea of a political *natio hungarica*, a notion that still held Bernolák's allegiance. In its stead they placed the cultural and linguistic nation (or 'tribe'), but Kollár understood by this the Czechoslovak nation, of which he considered the Slovaks an integral part. Finally, in the mid-1840s Štúr and other young Protestant intellectuals went still further: the Slovaks, they held, were neither part of a larger Czechoslovak cultural unity nor participants in a greater Hungarian political nation. They formed a Slavonic nation of their own, with its own language and a right to at least a measure of political autonomy (this last claim, however, was put forward publicly only in 1848).

The political implementation of theoretical nationhood was only achieved much later and as a result of the impact of external events. Slovak nationalism in the last quarter of the nineteenth century suffered a series of almost fatal blows. The small nationalist intelligentsia succeeded in maintaining itself then only with great difficulty. It was unable to prevent the increasing denationalization of the younger generation, chiefly by means of the school system, and it exercised scarcely any influence among the peasant masses who nevertheless preserved their Slovak language intact. From the beginning of the twentieth century the tide slowly began to turn, although perhaps too slowly to stay the gradual ebbing of Slovak national consciousness had the Hungarian state not disintegrated in 1918. But the winning of the masses for Slovak nationhood after that date could not have happened if a secure foundation for the idea of Slovak nationhood had not already been laid before 1848 by L'udovít Štúr and his predecessors in the national awakening.

# Notes

CHAPTER 1 THE DAWN OF SLOVAK NATIONALISM

1 Only two books have been devoted exclusively to the Slovak national awakening, one by a Marxist scholar, Butvin, *Slovenské národnozjednocovacie hnutie*, the other a rather brief study by a Hungarian writer, Wagner, *A szlovák nacionalizmus*. The latter is more an extended essay than a detailed exposition of the subject. The following works, though with wider coverage, also deal extensively with the national awakening; by exponents of the 'Czechoslovak' viewpoint: Hodža, *Československý rozkol*, and Pražák, *Dějiny spisovné slovenštiny*; by a Dutch scholar: Locher, *Die nationale Differenzierung und Integrierung*; by an exile Hungarian historian: Gogolák, *Beiträge zur Geschichte des slowakischen Volkes*, vols I and II. Hodža's book evoked a reply from the veteran Slovak historian Škultéty, *Sto dvadsat'pät*.

2 In the first half of the nineteenth century Protestant Slovaks formed roughly one-fifth and Catholics four-fifths of the Slovak-speaking population, which numbered nearly two million altogether. Some writers, however, give the Protestants a rather higher proportion, and estimates of the total Slovak population vary considerably too. See Bokes, *Vývin predstáv o slovenskom území*, p. 15; Novotný, *O bratrské družbě Čechů a Slováků*, p. 43; Arató, *A nemzetiségi kérdés*, vol. I, pp. 262, 263, 299-302. The overwhelming majority of Slovak Protestants were Lutherans, though a small group of Calvinist Slovaks, whose cultural life came under strong Magyar influence, existed in east Slovakia. See Pauliny, *Dejiny spisovnej slovenčiny*, pp. 412-15, for the latter's literary usage. In the Lutheran church of Hungary in the early nineteenth

century Slovaks made up about seven-tenths of the membership, the remainder being Magyars and Germans. Štúr, *Die Beschwerden und Klagen der Slaven*, p. 74

3 Pauliny, *Dejiny spisovnej slovenčiny*, p. 379-82
4 Rudolf Krajčovič, 'Hlavné fázy formovania kúltúrnej západoslovenčiny,' pp. 171-80, in *K počiatkom slovenského národného obrodenia*. See also two articles by Auty, 'The evolution of literary Slovak,' p. 148, and 'Dialect, *koiné*, and tradition,' pp. 343-4; Pauliny, 'Čestina a jej význam,' pp. 112, 114; Pišút, Rosenbaum, and Kochol, eds, *Literatúra národného obrodenia*, p. 40.
5 Mráz, *Dejiny slovenskej literatury*, pp. 56-7; Faith, 'Slovenské katolícki kazatelia'
6 For an understanding of the issues discussed here I found two works especially valuable (not least because they approach these issues from very different viewpoints): Rapant, *K počiatkom mad'arizácie*, and Szekfű, *État et nation*. Rapant's first volume covers the period from 1740 to 1790, the second the years 1790-2 when, after Joseph II's death, the first laws were passed by the Hungarian Diet making Magyar an official language (though as yet this was in practice limited to a very circumscribed area).
7 Cf. the following statement of this view: 'It would be incorrect to reduce Bernolák's linguistic usage to a simple codification, a linguistic reform. It is a question here of a qualitatively new concept of the Slovak language, closely connected indeed with the development of other elements of the nation and with the growth of national consciousness' (Tibenský, 'Počiatky slovenského národného obrodenia,' p. 533). See also the following articles by the same author: 'Bernolák's influence,' 'Ideológia slovenskej feudálnej národnosti,' 'K starším i novším názorom,' 'Formovanie sa ideológie slovenskej feudálnej národnosti.' Views of the kind expressed by Tibenský have been vigorously contested by Rapant (e.g. in 'K pokusom o novú historicko-filozofickú koncepciu,' p. 496).
8 See Tibenský, *J. Papánek – J. Sklenár*; Mráz, 'Zástoj cyrilometodejskej idey'; two articles by Tibenský, 'Vznik, vývoj a význam vel'komoravskej tradície,' and 'The function of the Cyril and Methodius and the Great Moravian traditions'; Butvin, 'The Great Moravian Cyril and Methodius tradition.'
9 Bernolák's philological treatises, including the two mentioned here, have been conveniently collected by Pavelek in a scholarly edition: see Bernolák, *Gramatické dielo Antona Bernoláka*.
10 Bernolák, *Bernolákovské polemiky*. See Kohuth, 'Jos. Ign. Bajza a slovenské prebudenie.'
11 Bajza, *René*. I have used Tibenský's edition published in Bratislava in 1955.

The first part was originally published in 1783, the second printed in 1785 but never distributed because of a ban by Bajza's ecclesiastical superiors who objected inter alia to his criticism of the monastic orders. In later years, however, he abandoned the 'enlightened' Catholicism of his youth.

12 Bernolák, *Bernolákovské polemiky*, pp. 159, 315, 316. Rapant argues that the basic cause of the acrimonious controversy between Bernolák and Bajza that broke out in the mid-1790s was not basically a question of disagreement on issues of philology. It stemmed primarily from the fact that 'Bajza war ihnen [i.e. Bernolák] zu weltlich, zu modern ... und zu josephinistisch' (*Slovenské povstanie roku 1848-49*, vol. V, pt 1, p. 198). This argument, while not improbable, is not backed by much concrete evidence. In general Rapant appears to me to overemphasize the confessional, anti-enlightenment elements which undoubtedly existed in Bernolák's *Weltanschauung* (e.g. see ibid., p. 197).

13 Bajza, *René*, pp. 283-6

14 Bajza's preface to *René*, p. 58; Kotvan, *Bernolákovci*, p. 27

15 See Zlatoš, *Písmo sväté u Bernolákovcov*, chap. 4; Ladislav Šášky, 'Bratislavský generálny seminár v bernolákovske hnutie,' pp. 97-112 in *K počiatkom slovenského národného obrodenia*.

16 A leading disciple of Bernolák, Canon Juraj Palkovič, wrote in 1827 concerning the six years' activity of the Bratislava general seminary: 'Fuit mandatum regium, ut materna lingua excoleretur et alumni etiam in scholis provocentur ad respondendum maternis linguis' (*Korešpondencia Jána Hollého*, p. 254).

17 Butvin, *Slovenské narodnozjednocovacie hnutie*, p. 44

18 One reply to the invitations sent out for support (*epistolae invitatoriae*) has been preserved. It was composed on 5 August 1786 by a middle-aged country parson, Ondrej Mészáros, who wrote: 'Ingratus certe esset in patriam suam, in nationem, linguam maternam, qui qualem potest ad opus isthoc symbolam non conferret. Ego ex parte mea, quidquid fieri poterit, lubens gratusque offero ... Slavonicam linguam quam cum lacte materno hausi, gratulabor, si vir ad 50-um properans ordinate ad regulas, vel ante mortem loqui et scribere potero.' The letter has been printed by Baník, 'Pomocníci Antona Bernoláka,' pp. 196-7. I am unable to see national consciousness – in the modern sense – in the use of the word *natio* (as here) or in the phrase *pannonio-slavica natio* (used by the seminarians themselves in another document dated 1790 and printed by Vyvíjalová, 'Snahy slovenských vzdelancov,' p. 241). These phrases refer to an ethnic group, not a national community; cultivation of the vernacular is the sole objective of these writers.

19 Auty, 'The evolution of literary Slovak,' pp. 149-50. I found Bartek, *Anton Bernolák*, a useful guide to Bernolák's linguistic reforms, and Mat'ovčík,

'Anton Bernolák. Zivot a dielo,' pp. 113-42 in *K počiatkom slovenského národného obrodenia*, a serviceable outline of his activities (see p. 122 for an opinion of Bernolák's relationship to the Enlightenment and Josephinism strikingly different from Rapant's view mentioned in n. 12 above). See also Habovštiaková, *Bernolákovo jazykovedné dielo*. The following works have been published in western languages: Úrhegyi, 'Un chapitre de l'histoire du langage littéraire slovaque,' and (less scholarly) J.M. Kirschbaum, *Anton Bernolák*. Another version of Úrhegyi's article has been printed in Hungarian: 'Bernolák Antal jelentősége.'

20 Almost all scholars agree that the year 1787, while certainly a landmark in the development of the Slovak language, did not constitute a violent break with the past. On this point, to give only one example, the Czech literary historian Jaroslav Vlček takes up a position identical to that of a strong Slovak nationalist, Ján Rekem; see Vlček, 'Anton Bernolák a jeho škola' [1890], reprinted in *Slovensku*, p. 250, and Rekem, *Slovak Literature and National Consciousness*, p. 36. Bernolák was more a 'codifier' of his predecessors' piecemeal efforts in slovakizing the literary language than a linguistic revolutionary, except perhaps in regard to orthography (see Auty, 'The evolution of literary Slovak,' p. 150).

21 Bernolák, *Gramatické diela*, p. 96

22 Ibid., pp. 118, 120, 128 (from his preface to his *Grammatica slavica* of 1789).

23 In a recent work, Vyvíjalová (*Bernolákov autentický slovníček*, pp. 26-30, 44, 45) has provided some good evidence of Bernolák's respect for the Czech language, despite his conviction that it should no longer act as the Slovak literary language.

24 Bernolák, *Gramatické diela*, p. 428 (from his preface to his *Etymologia vocum slavicarum* of 1791). See also Vyvíjalová, 'Snahy slovenských vzdelancov,' pp. 241-5.

25 The translation was carried out by Canon Palkovič on the prompting of Archbishop Rudnay of Esztergom after a resolution had been passed at a synod of the Hungarian church held in Bratislava in 1822 recommending that it be done; and it was published in two volumes in 1829-32. See Zlatoš, *Písmo sväté u Bernolákovcov*; Vyvíjalová, 'Alexander Rudnay,' and 'Snahy slovenských vzdelancov,' pp. 248-50; and also Hollý, *Korešpondencia Jána Hollého*, p. 81, for the poet's letter of appreciation to Palkovič for his efforts and, in particular, for providing a vernacular alternative to the Protestant translation into *bibličtina*.

26 Kotvan, *Juraj Fándly*, pp. 26, 108; Sedlák, *Strieborný vek*, vol. I, p. 285; Tibenský, 'Bernolák's influence,' pp. 173-4. On the Society's organization

see also the essays by Boris Bálent (pp. 189-200) and Michal Eliáš (pp. 213-20) in *K počiatkom slovenského národného obrodenia*, as well as Sedlák, *Strieborný vek*, vol. I, chap. 1, pt 2. Žatkuliak, *Juraj Fándli*, pp. 64-5, includes a map showing the location of the Society's sections and subsections. A list of its members was first published in Kohuth, 'Učené slovenské tovaryšstvo,' pp. 36-42. Kotvan in his biography of Fándly (pp. 83-103) reprints correspondence from the Society's archives, no longer extant, published by Fándly in his paper *Hospodár*, vol. III (1800). See also Tibenský's selection from Fándly's writings (Fándly, *Výber z diela*). Kotvan (pp. 131-6) gives a complete list of both Fándly's printed works and his extant unpublished writings.

27 One Protestant member, a pastor, is recorded. But, as Rapant remarks, 'Die angebliche Mitgliedschaft eines einsigen evangelischen Pfarrers ... ist daher viel eher als ein Beweis seiner, als der Gesellschaft überkonfessioneller Einstellung zu werten, falls es sich natürlich nicht um ungenügende Informiertheit, oder um einem Versuch einer Konversion handelt' (*Slovenské povstanie*, vol. V, pt 1, p. 201).

28 Tibenský, introduction to Fándly, *Výber z diela*, p. 87

29 Ibid., p. 49; Kotvan, *Juraj Fándly*, p. 72

30 Bajza was offended by Bernolák's critical attitude towards his Slovak usage. Nevertheless, he joined the Slovak Literary Society and remained on the fringe of the Bernolák movement until his death in 1836.

31 Quoted in Kotvan, *Juraj Fándly*, pp. 110-12

32 Letter to Fándly, 8 Feb. 1795, in ibid., p. 96. See also pp. 88, 89, 92, 95.

33 Ibid., pp. 95-7

34 Ibid., pp. 119, 121. See also Bobek, 'O historizme Fándlyho.'

35 Two works by Kotvan, *Bernolákovci* and *Bibliografia Bernolákovcov*, are especially useful. See also Mikuláš Bakoš, 'Poézia u bernolákovcov pred Hollým,' in *K počiatkom slovenského národného obrodenia*, pp. 221-40.

36 Ján Považan, 'Juraj Palkovič a jeho miesto v bernolákovskom hnutí,' in *K počiatkom slovenského národného obrodenia*, pp. 321-40, sets out the impressive contribution made by Palkovič to the movement. See also Banik, '180 rokov tomu čo sa narodil Juraj Palkovič.' Kútnik Šmálov, *Zástoj katolíckej hierarchie*, chaps 2 and 4, gives a highly flattering account of the Catholic hierarchy's role in promoting *bernoláčina*.

37 Vlček, *Kapitoly zo slovenskej literatúry*, p. 135

38 One of these dissidents was Štefan Moyses, the future bishop of Banská Bystrica, who in the 1860s became a leader of Slovak nationalism and supporter of *štúrovčina* (Brtáň, *Štefan Moyses*, pp. 16, 40-8). For an example of clerical indifference to *bernoláčina* see Chovan, 'Martin Hamuljak,' p. 18.

After 1848 we find a few Catholic clerics temporarily abandoning literary Slovak for an officially sponsored version of Czech; this, however, was largely due to political pressure from Vienna. But for the 1820s and 1830s 'there is indeed evidence that works destined for a wider Catholic public were ... published in Czech' (Pišút et al., *Dejiny slovenskej literatury*, vol. II, p. 121).

39 Vyvíjalová, 'Spolok milovníkov reči,' 'Snaha slovenských vzdelancov,' 'Snahy o jazykové zjednocovanie,' 'Snahy o založenie slovenských novín.' See the excellent biography, *Martin Hamuljak*, by Mat'ovčík, who has edited the first volume of Hamuljak's letters covering the years from 1824 to 1833 (Hamuljak, *Listy Martina Hamuljaka*). See also Butvin, 'Martin Hamuljak' (an earlier version was published in Slovak in *Historický časopis*, vol. XIII [1965], no. 4, pp. 517-45); Čechvala, 'Martin Hamuljak.' For the activities of Bernolák's supporters in east Slovakia from the 1820s, see Sedlák, *Strieborný vek*, vol. I, chap. 2, pt 2, and chap. 3, pt 3.

40 The last use of *bernoláčina* seems to have been in the *Katolické noviny* of 1851 ('Bernolákismu počiatok a koniec').

41 Úrhegyi, 'Un chapitre de l'histoire,' p. 182 (in Hungarian version on p. 467).

42 Rapant first put forward his views in his *Mad'arónstvo Bernolákovo*. Some forty years later his position remained unchanged; indeed it was, if anything, stated more rigorously (e.g. in his *Slovenské povstanie*, vol. V, pt 1, p. 202). The whole spirit of this preface, Rapant argued in 1930 (p. 13), was that of the eighteenth century: it could not have been composed, therefore, around 1825.

43 Chovan, ed., 'Predhovor'; Vyvíjalová, 'Novšie poznatky.'

44 Chovan, 'Predhovor,' p. 48

45 The Protestant editors of the Czech-language *Prešpurské noviny* welcomed the appearance of Bernolák's *Dissertatio* in 1787 and also printed several unsigned letters urging use of the vernacular in the paper. These were probably inspired, if not written, by Bratislava seminarians since we know the paper maintained contacts with them. Although the editors appear to have been sympathetic, the appeal did not arouse much response in the paper's readers. In the 1780s Slovak Catholics and Protestants on the whole took little notice of each others' literary endeavours; see Glassl, *Die slovakische Geschichtswissenschaft*, p. 110. We should note that the idea of using the vernacular for literary purposes had in the past been expressed by several Protestants, e.g. by Daniel Sinapius Horčička in the seventeenth century.

46 Letter from Ribay, 3 Sept. 1787, in Dobrovský, *Korrespondence*, vol. IV, p. 91. Dobrovský, who at first regarded Slovak as merely a dialectal variant of Czech, later changed his mind; while he continued to disapprove of *ber-*

*noláčina*, he came to allot Slovak a more independent status vis-à-vis Czech. See Hanuš, *Dobrovský a Slovensko*, pp. 15-18. Among Slovaks, both those who stood inflexibly on the basis of literary Czech and those who desired further slovakizing could draw support from Dobrovský's writings.

47 Letter from Ribay, 24 March 1786, in Dobrovský, *Korrespondence*, vol. IV, p. 34. See also Mráz, *Dejiny slovenskej literatury*, p. 112.

48 Quoted in Gogolák, *Beiträge*, I, p. 156. Cf. Palkovič's preface to his *Böhmisch-deutsch-lateinisches Wörterbuch*, vol. I, pp. vi, vii.

49 Whereas the German universities transmitted the ideas of the French Enlightenment to the Protestant intelligentsia, the Slovak Catholics obtained them via Vienna (Tibenský, 'Bernolák's influence,' p. 150). Štefánek ('Osvietenstvo na Slovensku,' pp. 19-20) suggests that the Catholics also got them via Hungary, and possibly direct from France.

50 To give just one example of this: the pastor and scholar Michal Semian states in the lengthy title of his history of Hungary, *Kratické hystorycké vypsánj*, written in Czech and published in Bratislava in 1786, that it was composed 'in the Slovak language (*w slovenském gazyku*),' whereas in the (unpaginated) preface he talks of 'our Slovak nation (*národ náš slovenský*)' clearly in reference to the Slovaks proper; moreover, Hungary was for him 'our dear fatherland (*naša milá vlast*).'

51 See Peukert, *Die Slawen der Donaumonarchie*, pp. 21-196, for an account limited to a single university, but an extremely important one in this connection.

52 Auty, 'The evolution of literary Slovak,' p. 152

53 For the controversy on this issue between the Catholic and the Protestant Palkovič, see Vyvíjalová, ed., 'Palkovičov preklad.'

54 Menčík, *Jiří Ribay*, pp. 27-9, 49-59. Ribay's Czechoslovak consciousness drew strength not only from the tradition of his church but also from the influence of the Czech and German Enlightenment and of Josephinism. Politically, however, he continued to be a Hungarian patriot like Bernolák. As part of his program of popular enlightenment, Ribay urged that Slovaks be taught to speak the colloquial language properly in addition to learning to write good Czech. See Szabó, 'A cseh-tót szellemi közösség kezdetei,' pp. 185, 186, 188, 193.

55 Vyvíjalová, *Juraj Palkovič*, pp. 103-28. The *gymnasium*, which in 1811 was promoted to the rank of *lycée* and whose upper classes in effect constituted the Lutheran church's theological seminary, had been founded in 1606. Although the school included a number of German- and Magyar-speaking students and its language of instruction was Latin, it nevertheless became an important centre of Protestant Slovak culture: Ján Čaplovič, 'Bratislavské

lýceum a slovenské národné obrodenie 1780-1830,' in *K počiatkom sloven-ského národného obrodenia*, pp. 285-302. Palkovič always lectured in Latin; only the Magyar language and literature and the Hungarian history classes were given in the vernacular as (since 1792) the law of the land required.

56 Kollár, in his memoirs, 'Paměti z mladších let života,' p. 202, describes Pal-kovič's neglect of teaching during the period when he was, at any rate nomi-nally, his pupil.

57 See Vilikovský, *Dějiny literárních společností malohontských*. Its activities continued, though with declining vigour, until 1842 (the other societies were comparatively shortlived). The Slovak Protestants of the mining districts of central Slovakia formed their own literary society in 1810 (Societas litteraria slavica montana); see Pražák, *Slovenské studie*, chap. 2. For the literary cul-ture of the Protestant Slovaks in general see Čapek, *Československá literatura toleranční*. Vol. I covers 1781-1818, vol. II 1818-61; since most Protestant literature in Czech was written by Slovaks, the book is largely concerned with Slovak literary production.

58 An example from the year 1814 is cited in Baník, 'Ján Hollý,' p. 28.

59 Vilikovský, *Dějiny literárních společností malohontských*, p. 86

60 Hirner, *Ján Feješ*, pp. 32-46, 60-7. See also Gogolák, *Beiträge*, vol. I, pp. 225-7.

61 A somewhat similar position was taken up by another Slovak Protestant of that period, Ján Čaplovič. Like Feješ, Čaplovič was a member of the minor Slovak gentry, and both men were scholars. Although Čaplovič was to reject Magyar as the state language more decisively than Feješ, he shared the latter's supranational Hungarian patriotism and support for linguistic equality be-tween the vernaculars. Like Feješ, he rallied to the defence of Slovak when its traditional position was threatened. In the pre-March era Čaplovič partici-pated actively in the Slovak Protestants' struggle against the Magyar liberal nationalist party in the Lutheran Church and wrote on their behalf, as for example in the pamphlet he published anonymously in Leipzig in 1842, *Slawismus und Pseudomagyarismus*. See his biography by Jankovič, *Ján Čaplovič*, esp. chap. 4. Both Čaplovič and Feješ publicly acknowledged their membership of the Slovak ethnic group – 'ich bin kein Magyare, und wünsche es auch nicht sein,' wrote Čaplovič in 1832 (quoted ibid., p. 96) – but this did not preclude their giving their national allegiance as noblemen to the Hungarian fatherland.

62 Some writers cite Jan Hrdlička's article, 'Wznessenost řžeči české neb wůbec slowenské,' published in a Protestant Czech-language newspaper, *Staré noviny*, in 1785, pp. 417-38, as an example of early cultural and linguistic nationalism. I do not accept this view. Although the article sings the praises

of 'our Slovak-Czech language' (p. 417) and reflects to some extent the interest in the Slovak past aroused by such works as Papánek's history, its author's position does not differ essentially from the prenational ethnic consciousness of Bernolák and his associates. It is interesting to note that, just as Bernolák in the preface to his dictionary was to recommend knowledge of literary Slovak as an aid in learning Magyar, so the editors of *Staré noviny* (in the article entitled 'Literatura slowanská, gest potřebná, a slaužj k rozssjřenj známosti řeči německé' [1785], esp. pp. 126-7) argued that an acquaintance with Czech literature would inspire Slovaks with a desire to get to know its German sources at first hand. See Škultéty, '*Staré Noviny* – Bernolák.' Much the same spirit as Hrdlička's infuses the verses in 'praise of the Slovaks,' published in 1791 by a Protestant student, Jiří Rohonyi. They have been reprinted in Tibenský, ed., *Chvály a obrany*, pp. 140-1.

63  In the preface (p. xi) to the first issue of the first volume of his paper, *Týdennjk, aneb Cýsařské kralowské národnj nowiny* (Bratislava). Two decades earlier, while a student at the University of Jena, he had composed a short essay, a rather pretentious and verbose little piece, in which some writers (e.g. Auty, 'Jan Kollár,' p. 87) have seen a possible influence of Herder's views on the Slavs – as given in his *Ideen zur Philosophie der Geschichte der Menscheit*, pt IV, bk XVI, chap. 4, which had recently appeared. Passages in the essay do indeed indicate a dawning consciousness of the cultural-linguistic concept of the nation. It was printed by Palkovič for the first time in 1817: 'Pogednánj.'

64  Palkovič's views on nationality seem to have been shared broadly by the Protestant poet Bohuslav Tablic who had been his fellow student at Jena in the early 1790s, although the evidence on the latter is not quite so clear. Tablic was certainly as ardent a Czechoslovak as Palkovič. In *Poezye*, vol. I, p. vi, he wrote: 'The Hungarian Slovaks who, together with the Moravians ... were once subject to the same monarch and have always considered themselves one and the same nation as the Czechs, today too ... must so consider themselves.' (See also his study 'O literních swazcích Slowákůw s Čechy a Morawany v nynější i někdejší době,' published posthumously in Prague first in *Časopis Českého musea* [1842] and then in Jan Kollár's collection, *Hlasowé* [1846]). And in his edition of the works of earlier Slovak poets, *Slowensstj werssowcy*, Tablic deliberately made his texts conform to standard Czech norms, thus eliminating his authors' slovakizing; see his statement to this effect in vol. II, p. 8. For this licence he was sharply criticized by Čaplovič in the preface to his own collection, *Slowenské wersse*, which Tablic's effort had inspired him to undertake. He wrote there: 'It is such a pity that he czechized all these verses, so much so that they are more Czech than Slovak ... I

have taken pains myself that as far as possible the verses I am printing should sound Slovak, just like our Slovaks talk ordinarily.' See also Miškovič, 'Tablic češtil!?' The language of Čaplovič's collection, however, is in fact not Slovak; it remains a slovakized Czech. We may note that Tablic, like Palkovič, approved of a limited amount of slovakizing when this occurred in works of a popular character. He maintained contact, too, with Hamuljak's circle in the Hungarian capital, hoping to convert them eventually from *bernoláčina* to *biblíčtina*.

65 The Slovak awakeners, especially during the first phase of the national revival (but later as well), were drawn largely from members of the two clerical intelligentsias; see Ján Hučko, 'Sociálne zloženie a pôvod slovenskej inteligencie v prvej fáze národného obrodenia,' in *K počiatkom slovenského národného obrodenia*, p. 52.

66 According to Szekfű, this stemmed from the identification made by Lajos Kossuth and his liberal followers of 'la frontière linguistique et la frontière de l'État, ce qui eût été une conséquence de l'idée française de nation' (*État et nation*, p. 208; see also pp. 14ff). This statement seems to me more plausible than Rapant's opinion that the Kossuthists, despite their liberal phraseology, were in fact primarily exponents of the old 'feudal' ideology, merely dressing it up to look like modern nationalism. While there were certainly traditional elements in the Kossuthist idea of nationality, essentially it derived from the territorial nationalism of western Europe. We should note that the Polish left around 1848 held views on this subject analogous to those of the Magyar liberal party. Of course, the fact that both Polish leftists and Magyar liberals were predominantly of gentry origin was not without influence in shaping their respective ideologies.

CHAPTER 2   SLOVAK NATIONALISM AND THE CZECHOSLOVAK IDEA

1 Cf. Čaplovič, *Gemälde von Ungarn*, vol. I, p. 220: 'Uebrigens ist kein Volk in Ungarn gegen seine Muttersprache so gleichgiltig, wie die Slowaken. Gebildetere schämen sich mit einander slowakisch zu sprechen, und bedienen sich immer des Lateins oder der deutschen Sprache. Dies ist bei Magyaren, Wlachen, Serben weniger der Fall.' He noted the ease with which Slovaks, especially educated Slovaks, were assimilated to Magyar culture.

2 The peasant uprising in north Hungary in 1831 resulted basically from social unrest and had no nationalist or panslav aims. See Rapant, *Sedliacke povstanie*. Slovaks formed the overwhelming majority of participants in the uprising.

3 *Über die literarische Wechselseitigkeit zwischen den verschiedenen Stämmen und Mundarten der slawischen Nation.* The year before Kollár had published a shorter version in Czech in *Hronka*, vol. I, no. 2, pp. 38-53, and Serb and Croat translations appeared in 1835 and 1836 respectively. He had already outlined his ideas on the subject early in the 1820s. The various versions of the treatise have been published under Miloš Weingart's editorship (Kollár, *Rozpravy*). See also Brtáň, *Vznik*, and, more generally, Arató, *A nemzetiségi kérdés*, vol. I, pp. 235-46.

4 Locher, 'Het Panslavisme,' pp. 151-3.

5 'Het is geen toeval, dat juist een Slovaak de voornaamste profeet van het panslavisme werd,' writes Locher (ibid., p. 150), pointing to the fact that consciousness of an ethnic identity separate from an all-Slav identity was less developed among the Slovaks than the Czechs. See also Pražák, 'The Slovak sources'; Kirschbaum, *Pan-Slavism*; Pražák, 'Kollárova myšlenka'; and Štefánek, 'Kollárov nacionalizmus.'

6 These thoughts are taken from Auty, 'Jan Kollár,' pp. 75, 76.

7 In one of his sermons he told his congregation: 'Don't take your name from the parts but from the whole of the nation. Never say, I am a Slovak, Moravian or Czech, Silesian, Pole, Serb or Croat. Say, I am a Slav! For the former weakens the feeling of its national greatness and tears the bond of unity' (Kollár, *Kázně a řeči*, vol. II, p. 624). In 1822 he preached two sermons which he published under the title *Dobré wlasnosti národu slowanského* (reprinted in *Kázně a řeči*, vol. I, pp. 497-524). In the first of these he enumerates the chief characteristics of 'the Slav nation': piety, industry, innocent enjoyment of life, love of the mother tongue, and tolerance. Of course large portions of his writing are infused with all-Slav messianism, and countless examples of this can be culled both from his prose and his verse. See also Haraksim, 'Od kollárova slovanství k slovenství (1835-1848).' Similar descriptions of the Slav character may also be found in many other slavophil writers of this period.

8 Rapant, *Slovenské povstanie roku 1848-49*, vol. I (*Slovenská jar 1848*), pt 1, p. 99. Elsewhere (vol. V, pt 1, p. 211) Rapant points to the immense appeal this new concept would possess for the Slavonic peoples of east-central Europe who, like the Slovaks, possessed neither state nor state tradition of their own. The panslav form in which Kollár presented it provided an added attraction since reliance on an imaginary 'Slavia' helped to compensate them for their own political weakness.

9 Quoted in Dolanský, 'Česko-slovenská spolupráce,' p. 137. For the primary role in nation-building that Šafařík allotted to language, see the introduction (almost certainly from his pen) to *Počátkové*, (1818) p. 41. Both men, of

course, regarded Czech, if not quite as their mother tongue, at least as their native literary language.

10 From Kollár's preface to *Pjsně swětské*, vol. I, p. xxiv. The volume appeared under the names of Šafařík, who was mainly responsible for its compilation, and Jan [Blahoslav] Benedikti, their colleague, whose role as editor was, however, nominal. A second volume appeared in 1827, this time anonymously and with a slightly altered title. Again the preface was Kollár's work; and he now took on the major editorial burden as well, with some help from Šafařík; see Škultéty, 'Kto sostavil prvý sväzok *Pjsní swetských.*'

11 They considered as premature the plan for creating a Slav *interlingua* of the kind elaborated by Ján Herkel' in his *Elementa universalis linguae slavicae* (Buda, 1826). Herkel' was a Catholic Slovak lawyer and a supporter of *bernoláčina*. For Herkel' see Mat'ovčík, 'Príspevok.'

12 Tóbik, *Šafárikov a Kollárov jazyk*, pp. 13, 68-78, and *passim*. According to Tóbik the period of most intensive slovakizing fell, for Kollár, within the years 1825-38, and for Šafařík, 1825-9. Tóbik (p. 76) attributes their eventual return to a more strict observance of Czech linguistic norms to growing fears of Magyar nationalism and of Slovak weakness. Šafařík's greater isolation from Slovakia, first in Novi Sad and then in Prague, made him the first to retreat.

13 Rosenbaum, *Pavel Jozef Šafárik*, p. 64

14 Kollár, 'Cestopis,' p. 246

15 Kollár, 'Myšlénky,' p. 47. See also Šafařík to Kollár, 18 May 1827, Šafařík, 'Dopisy,' vol. XLVIII, p. 285.

16 Both terms are applied to the Slovaks in Kollár's preface to *Pjsně swětské*, vol. II, pp. iii, xxviii. Of course Kollár's terminology, like that of almost all contemporary writers on the national question, was often inexact, indeed very confused.

17 Thus Kollár warmly supported the Illyrian movement since it fused all the South Slav peoples into a single 'tribe,' and he applauded the Great Russians' inclusion of the Ruthenian peoples in their 'tribe.' He also urged the Lusatian Serbs (i.e. Sorbs) to follow the Slovaks' example and adopt Czech as their literary language (see Kollár, 'Cestopis,' pp. 245-6, 264-5).

18 Kollár gives these arguments, for example, in his preface to *Pjsně swětské*, vol. I, pp. iii-xxiv. But two decades later he speaks of the Czechs as nearly twice as numerous as the Slovaks (see Kollár, 'Cestopis,' p. 264).

19 Vyvíjalová, 'Kollárov list,' and 'Snahy o jazykové zjednocovanie,' pp. 252-4; Butvin, *Slovenské národnozjednocovacie hnutie*, p. 117

20 Quoted in Rosenbaum, *Pavel Jozef Šafárik*, p. 44. Both he and Kollár were ardent folklorists throughout their lives.

21 Thus Votruba's claim in 'L'ud v bernolákovskej a v Štúrovskej reforme,' p. 66, that the publication of Kollár's two-volume collection of folk songs, *Národnie spievanky*, in 1834-5 marked the first appearance of modern literary Slovak in printed form seems to need some qualification. In the first place, Samo Chalupka has really a better claim to this distinction (see note 65 below). Secondly, several other collections of this kind had appeared earlier (though it is of course true that Kollár had inserted several folklike poems of his own into this collection, so that strictly speaking it was not purely a piece of folklore). Thirdly, the printing of oral literature in its vernacular form, as Kollár and Šafařík both recognized, was not tantamont to making a literary language out of the vernacular. At most, the sight of a printed page filled with a vernacular text in a book published under the sponsorship of a supporter of literary Czech must have made a striking impact on many readers. See the comment to this effect (but in reference to the first volume of *Pjsně swětské* which appeared in 1823) in Locher, *Die nationale Differenzierung und Integrierung*, p. 121. In any case Šafařík favoured a greater role for the vernacular in publications intended for the masses than in belles-lettres (Tóbik, 'Pavel Jozef Šafárik,' p. 223).

22 In a letter dated 14 Feb. 1821, Šafařík, 'Dopisy,' vol. XLVII (1873), p. 122

23 Šafařík to Kollár, 4 March 1823, ibid., p. 136. See also Minárik, 'Pavel Jozef Šafárik,' pp. 185-6.

24 Šafařík, *Geschichte*, pt II, chap. 2. In his list of the *slawische Sprachstämme* (p. 33) he omits the Bulgarians! Only after his history had appeared did he decide to separate them from the Serbs. See Rosenbaum, *Poézia*, pp. 33-64, for the background to this work's composition.

25 Šafařík, *Geschichte*, pp. 34, 375-79, 389, 390

26 Šafařík to P.I. Koeppen, 1 July 1825, *Korespondence*, vol. I (1927), p. 305

27 Šafařík, *Geschichte*, p. 389

28 Šafařík to Kollár, 18 May 1827, 'Dopisy,' vol. XLVIII (1874), p. 286; Šafařík to Palacký, 11 Oct. 1830 and 10 Jan. 1831, *Korespondence s Palackým*, pp. 90-1, 97-8

29 See, for example, Kollár to Palacký, 4 Oct. 1826, Palacký, *Korrespondence a zápisky*, vol. II, p. 284; Palacký to Kollár, 10 Jan. and 30 July 1827, Palacký, 'Dopisy,' pp. 388, 391

30 Kollár, 'Cestopis,' p. 246

31 Ms. by Kollár dated 1826 and cited in Šafařík, *Listy*, pp. 78-9; also Kollár's notes to his *Národnie spievanky*, vol. II, p. 568, and Rosenbaum, *Poézia*, pp. 202-4

32 See sources listed in previous chapter, n.39.

33 Šafařík to Hamuljak, 13 July and 9 Aug. 1829, Šafařík, *Listy*, pp. 163-4, 166, 167.
34 Hamuljak to Jungmann, mid-1827, Hamuljak, *Listy*, p. 87; Hamuljak to Šafařík, 6 Sept. 1827, ibid., pp. 93-5, 230
35 Ibid., p. 94. Hollý too was a Kollárian slavophil, as is demonstrated in a number of his poems, e.g. his *Básně*, vol. I, pp. 113-30, 191-7, 245-6, 253-4. Jozef Ambruš has pointed out, though, that the concepts 'Slovak' and 'Slav' often merge in Hollý's mind as they had done with his predecessors; see Ambruš, 'Die slawische Idee bei Ján Hollý,' in Holotík, ed., *L'udovít Štúr*, p. 47, and frequent comments to this effect in his edition of Hollý, *Korespondencia*. Hollý's poems were first collected and published in four volumes in 1841-2 in Buda as a result of the efforts of Hamuljak and his Society of the Lovers of Slovak Language and Literature.
36 Tomášik, 'Vlastný životopis,' p. 207, reports this fact in describing his meeting with Šafařík in Prague in 1834. Tomášik was author of the Slovak national hymn 'Hej Slováci!' which he originally composed in Czech. He took his inspiration for it from the Polish national anthem, 'Jeszcze Polska nie zginęła' (see ibid., p. 208).
37 Šafařík, *Slowanské starožitnosti*, p. 438. The previous year Šafařík had written to Kollár, warning him that what he was planning would kill Czech literature without doing the Slovaks any real good: We must 'preserve what we have and not begin anything new'; quoted in Novotný, *O bratrské družbě Čechů a Slováků*, p. 99.
38 Šafařík, *Slovanský národopis*, pp. 17, 90, 104, 146-7. See also Minárik, 'Pavel Jozef Šafárik,' pp. 203-4.
39 Kollár to Ctiboh Zoch, 12 Nov. 1836, Brtáň, ed., 'Z Kollárovej korešpondencie,' p. 220. Cf. the citation from Kollár dated 28 May 1836, on p. 186 of Butvin, *Slovenské narodnozjednocovacie hnutie*.
40 Kollár to Hanka, 9 April 1835, 'Vzájemné dopisy,' p. 237; Kollár, *Rozpravy*, p. 71. For Moravian linguistic separatism from the late 1820s see Hýsek, 'Dějiny.' Its exponents in fact did not advocate a complete break with Bohemian Czech but rather a Moravian presence within the common literary language such as Kollár and Šafařík desired in the Slovak vernacular. Kollár exercised some influence on the Moravian separatists but felt they went a little too far in questioning the basic unity of the constituent parts of the Czechoslovak community. The Moravian movement died away in the second half of the century, most of the leading figures in the Czech national revival strongly disapproving of it (see Novotný, *O bratrské družbě Čechů a Slováků*, p. 98)
41 Godra, 'Osvědčení,' *Zora*, vol. I (1835), pp. 282-4

42  Quoted in Butvin, 'Martin Hamuljak,' p. 164
43  Butvin, *Slovenské národnozjednocovacie hnutie*, pp. 188-9
44  Pišút, *Počiatky básnickej školy*, p. 242
45  Palkovič published many articles in *Tatranka* voicing his strong disagreement
    with the innovations recently introduced into Czech orthography and voca-
    bulary with the support of Jungmann, Palacký, etc. and expressing his fear
    of their subverting the younger generation in Slovakia: e.g. vol. I, pt 3
    (1834), pp. 101-15, and pt 4 (1837), pp. 99-119; vol. II, no. 1 (1841), pp.
    62-73. Palacký, too, had been Palkovič's pupil at the Bratislava *lycée*.
46  *Tatranka*, vol. II, no. 1 (1841), p. 72
47  *Hronka*, vol. I (1836), no. 2, pp. 38-9; see also no. 1, pp. 8-19.
48  Ibid., vol. II (1837), no. 1, p. 94. Kuzmány in the next decade became a
    supporter of *štúrovčina*: see Bujnák, *Dr Karol Kuzmány*, pp. 42-58, and
    articles by Rosenbaum, 'Vzt'ah Karola Kuzmányho,' and Kraus, 'Kuzmány
    a Štúrovci.'
49  These Polish contacts are discussed in Žáček, *Z revolučných ... stykov*, pp.
    19-106. For the Czech contacts, see Žáček, *Cesty českých studentů, passim*.
50  The late Ján Béder, though he did not invent the term 'Young Slovaks,'
    which was used by Slovak historians in the interwar period, helped to popu-
    larize it in his publications; see his 'Kollárova koncepcia,' and 'Nástup gene-
    rácie *Mladé Slovensko*.' Although there was no organizational link between
    the Young Slovaks and the contemporary Young Europe movement inspired
    by Mazzini, they shared ideas and sympathies and there may even have been
    some indirect contact between them. The most radical member of the group
    was Alexander Vrchovský, an enthusiastic polonophil who was at the same
    time a keen devotee of the Kollárian brand of slavophilism. For his slavophi-
    lism see his letter dated 17 Nov. 1837, printed by Béder, 'Spoločnost',' pp.
    72-4. Vrchovský also maintained contacts with German underground youth
    groups. *Zpráwa o ústawu slowanském*, pp. 3-4, illustrates the essentially re-
    formist character of their program.
51  Quoted in Brtáň, 'Slováci a Sreznevskij,' p. 129. There do not appear to be
    any grounds for the charge, first made by Karel Havlíček in 1846, that the
    linguistic schism of the mid-1840s resulted from the influence exercised on
    the Young Slovaks by slavophil scholars from Russia, especially Bodians'kyi
    and Sreznevsky, during visits to Slovakia in the late thirties or early forties.
    See Turcerová, 'Styky slavianofilov,' pp. 345-50; Stanislav, *Z rusko-sloven-
    ských kultúrnych stykov*, pp. 41-2; Novotný, *O bratrské družbě Čechů a
    Slováků*, pp. 145-52.
52  Quoted in Béder, 'Spoločnost',' p. 49.
53  Ibid., pp. 3-80, presents a detailed account of its history from 1835 to 1840,

the period when activities were at their height. In April 1837 Společnost, along with all other student societies at Protestant schools in Hungary, including the Magyar ones, were dissolved by the authorities who regarded them as potentially subversive. See Szekfű's introduction to *Iratok*. Szekfű points out rightly that this measure was directed in particular against the Magyar liberal nationalist movement. The more radically inclined members of Společnost continued activities in a clandestine organization, Vzájemnost, until about 1840 when it petered out. Meanwhile, Štúr and others had reactivated the moribund Slavonic Institute at the Bratislava *lycée*, which now became a focus for Slovak student efforts.

54 Sedlák, in the second volume of *Strieborný vek*, prints a copious selection of documents concerning the Slovak student societies at Prešov (pp. 19-102), Levoča (pp. 103-209), and Kežmarok (pp. 210-28). See also vol. I, chap. 2, pt 4, *passim*.

55 See article 2 of regulations of the Bratislava *lycée*'s Slovak society (1829), printed in Bakoš, *L'udovít Štúr*, p. 207. The term 'Czechoslav' stemmed from the students' strong slavophil sentiments.

56 Ferienčiková, ed., *Knižnica*, pp. 13-73, contains a short history by Mária Vyvíjalová of the library available to the Slovak students at the Bratislava *lycée*. This library came into existence in 1827 and included many books in Slav languages other than Czech or Slovak, a reflection of the students' slavophil sympathies.

57 Hurban, *L'udovít Štúr*, pp. 88-100; Goláň, *Štúrovské pokolenie*, p. 28. See also Hurban, *Slovensko*, pp. 207-8. The Young Slovaks' discovery of the Great Moravian tradition resulted in large measure from their reading Hollý's epic poems, *Svatopluk* (1833) and *Cyrilo-Metodiáda* (1835); see 'Veľkomoravská a cyrilometodejská tradícia u Štúrovcov,' unsigned contribution in *Veľká Morava*, pp. 140, 159. The adoption of Slavonic names was imitated by young Slovak nationalists elsewhere too.

58 Škultéty, *Sto dvadsat'pät rokov*, pp. 33-4. For the situation at the Protestant college in Prešov see Záborský to František Cyril Kampelík, 26 Feb. 1834, printed in Lazar, *Jonáš Záborský*, pp. 223-4, and, for the situation in the later 1830s at the *lycée* in Levoča, Viktorin, 'Ján Kalinčak,' pp. 107-8.

59 For an excellent example of this see the Bratislava students' letter to Hollý, 3 Oct. 1835, in Hollý, *Korešpondencia*, p. 107.

60 See, for example, Hurban to Václav Staněk, 25 July 1838, in Hurban, 'Dva listy Miloslava Jozefa Hurbana,' p. 89. For contacts between young Bernolákites and Young Slovaks see Butvin, 'Tajny politický spolok,' pp. 17-21, 23-4.

61 *Plody*, pp. 60-5, 70-2

62 Jóna, 'Učast' Ľudovíta Štúra,' p. 133; Hurban, *Ľudovít Štúr*, pp. 62, 82

63 Štúr to Godra and Palacký, 4 and 10 April 1836, in Štúr, *Listy*, vol. I, pp. 56-7, 61

64 Vlček, *Dejiny*, pp. 110-13

65 In three poems published in 1834 in Fejérpataky's *Nowý i starý wlastenský kalendár*. One of them, 'Nad Tatrou sa nebo kalí,' had been written as early as 1832. See the following articles in *Slovenské pohľady*: Škultéty, ed., 'Slovenské piesne'; Krčméry, 'Prielom Sama Chalupku,' and 'Prielom štúrovských básníkov.' Sedlák, *Strieborný vek*, vol. I, pp. 89-91, discusses the work of a Protestant pastor, Andrej Čorba, who early in the 1830s was writing in east Slovak. But his work, an eye-witness account of the peasant uprising of 1831, though intended for publication, was never in fact printed, and it had no successors.

66 For example, Chalupka to Vrchovský, 6 Aug. 1839, *Slovenské pohľady*, vol. XXI (1911), no. 6, p. 382

67 Hroboň to F.L. Rieger and A.J. Vrťátko, 14 Aug. 1838, quoted in Kleinschnitzová, *Andrej Sládkovič*, p. 293. A report by P.V. Ollík, 23 Oct. 1837 (quoted in Butvin, *Slovenské národnozjednocavacie hnutie*, p. 227) contrasts the average reader's hostility towards books written in 'high Czech' to the avidity with which works published in a slovakized Czech were consumed. Butvin (ibid., p. 229) gives further examples of this attitude among the Young Slovaks. In 1841 Štúr, in his capacity as assistant editor of *Tatranka*, observing that the paper's readers often complained of difficulty in understanding Czech words used in its columns, promised, if they sent in lists of words that gave them trouble, to print a short vocabulary explaining their meanings.

68 Vyvíjalová, 'Snahy o založenie slovenských novín,' pp. 133-61. The phrase cited is from p. 155.

69 Quoted in Mrlian, *Jozef Miloslav Hurban*, p. 25

70 *Kwěty*, vol. VI, no. 43, 24 Oct. 1839, p. 344. Štúr complained bitterly of the unwillingness of the Prague intelligentsia to practise 'literary reciprocity' towards the Slovaks. They were uninterested in Slovak culture, he declared during a visit to the Bohemian capital (in a letter dated 13 October 1838; *Listy*, vol. I, p. 160). Holly's poems, he observed, were scarcely known in Prague and the same went for Kollár's *Národnie spievanky*, the reason for all this being that 'our speech is offensive to them.'

71 For example in his letter, 22 Nov. 1840, printed in Jan Cimrák, 'Dva listy Kollárovy Samoslavu Hroboňovi,' in Pastrnek, ed., *Jan Kollár*, p. 56

72 The Czech-Slovak *rozkol* and its impact on the development of Slovak nationalism are discussed in the next chapter.

73  Gogolák, *Beiträge*, vol. II, p. 191. The first target of the Magyar liberals'
onslaught, the volume of poems written by students at the Levoca *lycée*,
*Jitřenka*, was an entirely Kollárian production both in content and in language. The faculty member most responsible for its publication, Professor
Michal Hlaváček, was a disciple of Kollár, and he continued to be loyal to
the Czechoslovak idea after the emergence of *štúrovčina*; see Pražák, *Literární Levoča*, pp. 27-36, 58-69, and *passim*. For Kollár's influence on the
contributors to *Jitřenka*, see Marták, 'Poézia,' pp. 47-83. Their language was
Czech – or perhaps one should say Czechoslovak – but of the artificial, bookish kind fostered by Kollár. Gogolák, *Beiträge*, vol. II, pp. 176-7, points out
that among the contributors were sons of Magyar gentry, mostly from east
Slovakia, who had succumbed to the spell of Slovak nationalism while at
school. (At home, of course, it is true they must have been familiar with
Slovak as well as Magyar, since both languages were widely spoken in the
region.) On the other hand, in the Protestant secondary schools of northern
Hungary teachers of Slovak background were to be found in this period in
the Magyar liberal as well as the Czechoslovak camp (Ibid., p. 182).

74  Jungmann to F. Šír, 13 March 1838, quoted in Butvin, *Slovenské národnozjednocovacie hnutie*, p. 228

75  Kollár to Staněk, 19 May 1844, in Kollár, 'Některé listy,' pp. 189-91

76  Quoted in Pražák, *Dějiny spisovné slovenštiny*, p. 379

77  *Hlasowé o potřebě jednoty spisowného jazyka pro Čechy, Morawany a
Slowáky*. By comparing the printed texts with the original manuscripts
Hendrich, in 'Hlasové,' has shown that Kollár tampered with a number of
the contributions. He toned down, or omitted altogether, passages that gave
qualified approval to *štúrovčina* (see ibid., pp. 377-84). For Šafařík's role in
the undertaking and his attitude to *štúrovčina* and its supporters, see Paul,
*Pavel Josef Šafařík*, pp. 260-3; Rosenbaum, *Pavel Jozef Šafárik*, pp. 137-51;
Vlček, 'Kterak Šafařík smýšlel,' pp. 302-6; Volf, 'Kollár,' pp. 292-3; Béder,
'Pavel Jozef Šafárik,' pp. 267-93; Novotný, 'K vzájemnému vztahu.' Šafařík
has usually been considered as more moderate in his opposition to *štúrovčina* than Kollár (he was certainly so regarded by Štúr and his friends). But
Novotný (ibid., pp. 50-3) questions this. The tone of Šafařík's contribution
to *Hlasowé*, which was what the *štúrovcy* read, was indeed restrained. But
other evidence indicates that he backed Kollár to the hilt in his campaign
against them. Certainly his comments to Bodians'kyi, penned in 1845 and
1846 (Šafařík, *Korespondence*, vol. I, pp. 93, 99, 100, 103), show he reacted
strongly against the schism, though he dismissed as absurd the view that it
had resulted from the machinations of Russian slavophil scholars (p. 103).

78 *Hlasowé*, pp. 65, 68-9, 77-80, 82-3. Kollár, though he did not dismiss the idea completely, was now much less enthusiastic than he had earlier been concerning a Slovak presence within the joint language. He wrote (*Hlasowé*, p. 230): 'In the final analysis we are not opposed to Czechoslovak language and literature taking special account of the Slovak people, its speech, its needs and its capabilities, in certain books and papers.' Unlike Šafařík he opposed any suggestion of two literary forms: one for use in church and *belles-lettres* and the other in publications for the people.

79 Ibid., pp. 154, 158, 167

80 Ibid., p. 71

81 Ibid., p. 190

82 Rapant, *Slovenský prestolny prosbopis*, vol. I, p. 241, vol. II, pp. 612-15

83 Frantsev, 'Štúrovo "schisma" a jeho ohlasy,' no. 3, p. 204. For sympathetic reaction to *štúrovčina* on the part of a small number of Czech intellectuals see ibid., pp. 201-6. But Havlíček, came out strongly against it in 1845-6, although he did not contribute to *Hlasowé* (see ibid., no. 2, pp. 101-4). Frantsev also published an account of the linguistic schism in Russian, *Chesko-slovenskii raskol*, but it does not differ substantially from the Czech version.

84 László Sziklay, *Launer István*, discusses Launer's career as well as his publications of 1847 and 1848 and their intellectual background.

85 See *Gitřenka*, pp. 21-2, 27-8.

86 Marták, in *Útok*, deals in detail with Launer's and Lanštják's publications directed against *štúrovčina* and accuses both men of being national renegades (though he considers Lanštják may only have been an unconscious dupe of the Magyars, p. 27). He goes on to argue that even before March 1848 their aim was not so much to support Kollár as to further the ends of magyarization (p. 11). This last argument sounds thoroughly implausible. Though it is true that in 1848 they both took the Magyar side, in fact many conservative Slovak Lutherans (such as Seberini) did this too. Their stand may have resulted in part from fear, should they favour the Slovak nationalists backed by Vienna, of losing the support of the county authorities who were often strong Magyar nationalists; see Rapant, 'Nastolenie spisovnej slovenčiny,' p. 26. But Sziklay, (*Launer István*, pp. 39-42, 54-5, 59) has shown in Launer's case (and Seberini's as well) that support of the Magyar cause in 1848 was combined with continued adherence to Czechoslovak cultural nationalism. I have dealt with a similar example of a split between political and cultural allegiance in my study of the Galician Ukrainian awakener, Ivan Vahylevych, first published in *Canadian Slavonic Papers* (Ottawa), vol. XIV (1972),

no. 2, pp. 153-90, and then in my book *Nationalism and Populism in Parti-tioned Poland*, London, 1973, pp. 102-41. In 1848 Vahylevych declared in favour of the Polish side while remaining a Ukrainian (Ruthenian) cultural nationalist. Vahylevych identified Polish political nationalism with the cause of liberty in the same way as Launer and others identified the Magyar na-tionalists' struggle against Vienna with freedom. For Launer and Lanštják see also Gogolák, *Beiträge*, vol. II, pp. 229-30.

87 Accusations of desertion, treachery, and apostasy have been levelled against the two leading representatives of this trend, Kollár and Šafařík, e.g. by Pola-kovič, *Začiatky*, p. 26. Such charges appear to me absurd: they reflect, not serious scholarly opinion, but the aberrant nationalism displayed in recent times only too frequently by academics in many parts of the world. In this case, as Ferenc Wagner has pointed out, 'since the Kollár who acknowledged all Slavdom as his nation was also an adherent of independent Slovak intel-lectual development, he, too played – just because of this fact – an important, almost indeed an innovative (kezdeményezö) role in forming Slovak national consciousness' (*A szlovak nacionalizmus*, p. 32).

### CHAPTER 3 THE MAKING OF A SLOVAK NATION

1 The most useful general accounts of this transformation are to be found in the relevant sections of Butvin, *Slovenské národnozjednocovacie hnutie*, and Gogolák, *Beiträge*, vol. II. Gogolák has also published a third volume cover-ing the period from 1848 to 1919 (1972).

2 No study of Štúr's life and thought that is both detailed and scholarly has appeared since the publication of Tourtzer, *Louis Štúr*. But this work of course is long out of date. Probably the most thorough of a number of popu-lar biographies is Sojková, *Skvitne ešte život*, a translation from the Czech. Hurban, *L'udovít Štúr*, originally published in 1881-4 and recently issued in an edition by Jozef Štolc, remains a valuable source of information on both Štúr and his movement. See also *L'udovít Štúr: Život a dielo*, a collection of essays. In English there is only Kirschbaum, *L'udovít Štúr*.

3 Gogolák, 'A szlovák és ruszin nemzetiség története,' pp. 254, 263. In his introduction to *Iratok*, p. 124, Szekfű describes the view of many Magyar nationalists, that the Slovaks (in contrast to the Magyars themselves) did not properly constitute a nation, as 'the product of the estates way of thinking. Applied to the modern nationality question, however, [such opinions] strengthened the nation-state concept.' Szekfű's long introduction to *Iratok* (pp. 5-208) traces in detail the history of the struggle to establish Magyar as

the official language of Hungary. Among the most essential of the 170 documents collected by Szekfű are nos 12 (1791), 27 (1792), 36 (1805), 81 (1830), 120 (1836), 132 (1840), 164 (1844). They reprint the texts of articles in the Diet decrees relating to the (gradual) introduction of Magyar as the language of the Hungarian state. The first three are in Latin, the last three in Magyar.

4 This has been the subject of a monograph by Rapant, *Ilegálna mad'arizácia*, which contains extensive documentation.

5 Gogolák, 'A szlovák,' p. 265; Rapant, *Slovenské povstanie*, vol. I, pt 1, pp. 66-70; Július Mésároš, 'Magyaren und Slovaken: Zur Frage des Panslavismus in der Vormärzzeit,' in Holotík, ed., *L'udovít Štúr*, p. 189. Mésároš's article was originally printed in *Jahrbücher für Geschichte Osteuropas* (Wiesbaden), NS, vol. XV (1967), no. 3, pp. 393-414.

6 The conservative group led by Count Janos Mailáth, and its press organ *Nemzeti ujság*, were also well disposed towards the Slovaks' cultural aspirations.

7 Arató, *A nemzetiségi kérdés*, vol. I, p. 138: 'The struggle waged for the Magyar language pointed the way for the Slovaks and stimulated them to strive more boldly for the emancipation of their own language ... The Slovaks then, just like the Croats and Serbs, utilizing the example of the Magyars and animated by it, fought against magyarization, which ... hindered, and indeed threatened, the cultivation and development of their tongue.'

8 Cf. Štúr, *Die Beschwerden und Klagen der Slaven*, p. 25

9 In addition to Magyars, the Magyar party included Germans who sympathized with its liberalism or had become assimilated to Magyar culture and also some Slovaks. An example of the latter is the scholar Ladislaus Bartholomacides. He always declared his loyalty to the Slovak ethnic group and upheld the use of the mother tongue in everyday life. 'Ich bin meiner slavischen Nation zugethan' he wrote. And he never learnt to speak Magyar well. Yet he supported the Magyar party within his church in its conflict with the Slovak nationalists, whom he regarded in general as 'panslavs.' And he asserted his membership of the Magyar 'state-nation': 'Ein jeder ... in Ungarn legaliter ansässige Slawe ist ein Ungar oder Magyar.' See his biography by Adamovič, *Ján Ladislav Bartholomoeides*, pp. 20-3. Bartholomaeides represents a fusion of ethnic loyalty with Hungarian patriotism frequently to be found among educated Slovaks of both denominations up into the interwar years of the twentieth century.

10 See Oberuč, 'Črty z dejín,' pp. 42-7. Szekfű, in *État et nation*, p. 200, writes of 'le malheureux projet de magyarisation de l'Église luthérienne slovaque, émis par le comte Zay.' This judgment is echoed by Domokos Kosáry, 'A

Pesti Hirlap nacionalizmusa 1841-1844,' *Századok* [Budapest], vol. LXXVII [1943], no. 3/4, p. 394: 'It was in truth an unfortunate policy to pursue a plan of this kind ... The Magyar nationality was in no way strengthened as a result, whereas it unnecessarily sharpened the [Slovaks'] hostility and provided ammunition for the enemies of Magyar nationalism.' See also Arató, *A nemzetiségi kérdés*, vol. II, pp. 46-8, 115-20; Kosáry, 'A Pesti Hirlap nacionalizmusa,' pp. 392-8.

11 Mésároš, 'Magyaren und Slovaken,' p. 193 (see note 5)

12 E.g. Michal Miloslav Hodža, *Der Slowak*, p. 50: 'Sonst ein grundehrlicher Mann, aber in Artikel des Magyarismus das blindeste Werkzeug jeder Partei,' i.e. the Magyar liberals.

13 The citations (except for the first) are all taken from an open letter from Zay to the slavophil professors of the Protestant *lycée* in Levoča, 24 Nov. 1840. It is printed in German translation in Zay's *Protestantismus*, pp. 61-5, and Chalupka published an almost identical version in *Schreiben*, pp. 5-10. Both pamphlets were published anonymously in Leipzig in 1841. The first reference to 'our Slav brethren' is from Zay, *Protestantismus*, p. 70.

14 Pulszky to Count Thun, 24 April 1842, printed in Thun, *Die Stellung der Slowaken*, pp. 4-5. Thun, a Bohemian aristocrat, was sympathetic to the Slav cause both in his own land and in north Hungary.

15 Chalupka, *Schreiben*, p. 35

16 Letter from Štúr, 13 March 1841, in Štúr, *Listy*, vol. I, p. 216

17 Ormis has reprinted many of them in Slovak translation in *O reč a národ*; see his introduction (pp. 11-165) and also his article 'Slovenské národné obrany.' For a specimen of this type of political literature from the Catholic side see Augustín Mat'ovčík, 'Neznáma národná obrana Jána Herkel'a z roku 1826.' *Historické štúdie* (Bratislava), vol. XIV (1969), pp. 223-36.

18 See, for example, Hoič, *Sollen wir Magyaren werden?* pp. 16-17, and *Apologie*, p. 18; Šuhajda, *Der Magyarismus*, pp. 3-8, 11ff, 19, 51.

19 Milan Hodža, *Československý rozkol*, p. 159, cites an example of this from the report of a Hungarian censor dated February 1843: 'Patria Hungarum et Slavorum una est et ideo ... distinctio patriae Slavicae [i.e. Slovak] et zelus pro eadem ad typum non admittitur ... Procavenda erit nominatio Slavicae nationis.' In a letter to the Russian slavist Sreznevsky, 8 May 1843 (*Listy*, vol. I, p. 356), Štúr wrote: 'The censorship allows nothing of ours through, for it is in the hands of the Magyars and they won't even allow us to grouse.'

20 The publication in 1842 of a new hymnbook in *bibličtina* also helped to emphasize the separateness of the Slovaks within a church that included Magyar and German members. It was based on earlier collections (especially

the Czech exile Jiří Tranovský's *Cithara sanctorum*, 1636) and incorporated much of the spiritual heritage of the Slovak Protestants, thus reinforcing their national identity. It was no accident that it appeared at a time when this identity was being challenged by Magyar 'liberal' churchmen. See Rapant, 'Predzpěvníkové polstoročie.'

21 See the definitive work by Rapant, *Slovenský prestolny prosbopis*. The first volume contains the author's narrative; the second prints the documents on which it is based.

22 Even so, a Magyar nationalist journal, *Társalkodó*, branded the more narrowly based petition that finally emerged as the work of 'panslav clergymen'; see Mésároš, 'Magyaren und Slovaken,' pp. 215-16 (see note 5).

23 Rapant, *Slovenský prestolny prosbopis*, vol. I, pp. 125ff, 136-43; vol. II, pp. 397-401, 580-6

24 Ibid., vol. I, p. 280 ('Zusammenfassung'): 'Die Überzeugung, dass man sich nur auf die eigenen, hauptsächlich völkischen Kräfte verlassen kann, lenkte die führenden slowakischen Politiker von der ergebnislosen versuchten hohen Politik auf die weit wichtigere Kleinarbeit der völkischen Sammlung. Diese Erkenntnis war die bedeutsamste Lehre der Wiener Unternehmung und wurde in weiteren allmählich zum allgemeinen Wahlspruch der slowakischen Bewegung.' Cf. Gogolák's view that the Slovak nationalists' failure to develop a state-oriented ideology before 1848 was a tragedy for the Slovaks since it fatally weakened their impact on the Hungarian scene (Gogolák, 'Die historische Entwicklung,' pp. 60-1). But to me it scarcely seems realistic to expect such an ideology to emerge among the Slovaks in that period.

25 Štúr, *Das neunzehnte Jahrhundert*, p. 13. We may remark that in this pamphlet Štúr did not attempt to justify the internal policies of Austria and her allies; he defended only their cultural politics. And Greeks and Serbs, for instance, did indeed look to Russia at this time to help liberate them from the Turks, while the non-Magyar nationalities of Hungary, we have seen, looked to the Habsburg monarch for protection against threatened denationalization (see Rapant, 'Nastolenie spisovnej slovenčiny,' p. 24).

26 Historians of the 'Czechoslovak' school have tended in general to exaggerate the political element when discussing the linguistic schism of the mid-1840s. See, for example, Milan Hodža (a Slovak), *Československý rozkol*, pp. 289, 291, and Pražák (a Czech), *Dějiny spisovné slovenštiny*, pp. 352-3. Cf. Škultéty, *Sto dvadsatpät rokov,'* passim, and Locher, *Die nationale Differenzierung und Integrierung,'* pp. 163-7, for criticism of their viewpoint.

27 See Škultéty, 'D'ord' Kossuth.'

28 The two petitions are printed in Vyvíjalová, *Slovenskje Narodňje Novini*, pp. 173-9.

29 Schulek, 'Une famille de Haute-Hongrie,' helps to illuminate the complex
national loyalties of the minor Slovak nobility of this period by taking as a
case study a Protestant family called Šulek with its German (Schulek) as well
as Magyar (Sulyok) branches. At mid-century it contained 'des représentants
de toutes les conceptions existant en Hongrie: Allemand d'espirit hongrois,
Autrichien partisan de la dynastie, pan-Slave condamné à mort, illyrien de
grande culture et *honvéd* magyarisant son nom' (pp. 143-4).

30 Rapant, 'Nastolenie spisovnej slovenčiny,' pp. 16-17

31 Ibid., pp. 16-22

32 From Francisci's letter, 28 Jan. 1843, in Milan Hodža, *Československý
rozkol*, p. 140. One of Štúr's former students, Jozef Podhradský, claimed
that the example of the Serb awakener Vuk Karadžić, who published in the
folk speech, influenced a hesitant Štúr and led him finally to follow suit (see
Ormis, ed., *Súčasníci*, p. 181). From 1843 onwards, relations between Štúr's
group and Gaj and his 'Illyrians,' which had previously been friendly, began
to deteriorate. Štúr now regarded Illyrianism as an 'abstraction' which cut its
adherents off from the people (Štúr, *Listy*, vol. I, pp. 343, 357), whereas
some – though not all – Illyrians were hostile to *štúrovčina*. See Matula,
'Mladé Slovensko,' and Novotný, 'Ke krizi Čechoslovakismu'; also Klatík,
'Ilyrské hnutie.'

33 Hučko, *Michal Miloslav Hodža*, and Mrlian, *Jozef Miloslav Hurban*, are useful
for the activities of the two men who, after Štúr, were most responsible for
the new Slovak nationalism.

34 Jóna, 'Účast' L'udovíta Štúra,' p. 136. After the linguistic schism had become public many of its supporters continued for a time to use *bibličtina* in
sermons and strictly religious publications. Ctiboh Zoch was one of those
who from the very beginning employed the new literary language for these
matters as well as for secular literature (see Palkovič, 'Ctiboh Zoch,' p. 324).

35 Hurban, in *Cesta Slováka*, speaks in this sense on several occasions (e.g. pp.
80, 96). He expressed the idea as late as the first half of 1842; see Hurban,
'Myšlénky a zprawy ze Slowenska o Slowensku,' *Nowiny z oboru literatury,
uměnj a wěd*, Supplement to *Kwěty* (Prague), vol. IX (1842), no. 10 (18
May), pp. 37-40; no. 11 (1 June), pp. 43, 44. Pražák, *Slovenská otázka*, pp.
21-6, shows how steeped in Czech culture was the young Hurban.

36 Hurban to Škultéty, 27 Dec. 1842, in Novotný, *O bratrské družbě Čechů a
Slováků*, pp. 184-5

37 For the views of Hurban and other young supporters of new Slovak at this
time see Helcelet, *Korrespondence*, pp. 578, 590. Helcelet visited Hurban in
August 1843. For Hurban see also his diary of this period published in *Ňitra*,
vol. II (1844), pp. 235-40. Elsewhere Hurban wrote: 'The spark of Slavdom

can appear in the people only after the spark of its own being, Slovakia, has appeared' (from his preface to Červenák, *Zrcadlo Slowenska*, pp. xv, xvi). Červenák, a member of Štúr's circle, died in 1842 at the age of twenty-six and his book was published posthumously. He composed the work in a 'Czechoslovak' spirit but Hurban's preface expressed the 'separatist' viewpoint: both preface and text, however, were written in Czech.

38  Goláň, *Štúrovské pokolonie*, p. 116
39  Lehocká to Rajská, 12 Nov. 1843, Lehocká, 'Listy,' p. 151. See also Hroboň to Staněk, 26 Sept. 1843, in Novotný, *O bratrské družbě Čechů a Slováků*, p. 196; Štúr to Staněk, 19 June 1844, in Štúr, *Listy*, vol. II, pp. 42-3; and many other examples of this attitude. Some supporters of the Slovak vernacular looked forward to an eventual reuniting of the Czech and Slovak languages in a new literary Czechoslovak, e.g. the poet Samo Tomášik ('Listy Sama Tomášika,' pp. 9, 10). The Lutheran church leader Pavel Jozeffy gave qualified support to a literary vernacular only after expressing his hope for a return to 'Czechoslovak' when use of the vernacular had done its job in raising the level of popular culture.
40  Auty, 'Dialect,' pp. 340, 342, 343, and 'The evolution of literary Slovak,' pp. 154-5; Pauliny, *Dejiny spisovnej slovenčiny*, p. 394. See also two contributions on *štúrovčina* in *L'udovít Štúr*, by Jóna (pp. 197-213) and Habovštiak (pp. 315-21). In addition I have found Bartek, 'L. Štúr a slovenčina,' useful.
41  Hroch, *Die Vorkämpfer*, p. 116. Hroch's analysis of the Slovak 'patriotic intelligentsia' from the 1820s to the 1840s (pp. 112-16) is based on the researches of Ján Hučko, which remain unpublished at the end of 1973.
42  The first publication to appear entirely in new Slovak was Francisci, *Svojim vrstovňikom na pamjatku*. Containing a mere six pages of verse, it was printed in Bratislava early in 1844 under the pseudonym Janko Rimarski. In the spring of the same year Hurban brought out the second volume of his literary almanac *Nitra*; whereas the first volume had been written in Czech, the second was published in new Slovak with a dedication to D'ord' Kossuth. For the background to its publication and for its significance in the emergence of new Slovak, see Pišút, *Literárne štúdie a portrety*, pp. 54-69. Although several other young writers later to win distinction were already at work in new Slovak, the first to publish something of lasting value was Andrej Sládkovič, with his romantic poem, *Marína*, in 1846. A marked increase in the size of the editions of some works in new Slovak, compared to previous Slovak publications in Czech (Milan Hodža, *Československý rozkol*, p. 266), indicates its popularity at least among members of the Protestant intellectual elite.

43 E.g. Tomásik, 'Listy Sama Tomášika,' pp. 7-9, 14, 29

44 See Jóna, 'Účasť' M.M. Hodžu.'

45 Štúr, *Nárečja slovenskuo alebo potreba písaňja v tomto nárečí.* Here *nárečja* (*nárečie* in the modern spelling) is translated as 'tongue' instead of the more exact 'dialect.' Štúr's objective in this treatise was to prove that Slovak was an independent language and not a dialect of Czech; to use the term 'dialect' might therefore prove misleading. In the same year, 1846, Štúr published a grammar of new Slovak, *Nauka reči slovenskej*, reprinted in *Dielo*, vol. V, pp. 151-253.

46 Rapant, 'Doba štúrovská,' p. 136.

47 Štúr, *Nárečie slovenské*, p. 7

48 Štúr, *Dielo*, vol. V, p. 11, and *Die Beschwerden und Klagen der Slaven*, pp. 1, 2, 6-8. From this view stemmed the intense interest in folklore, and especially in the collection of folk songs, displayed by Štúr himself and other members of his movement (e.g. Ján Francisci, Pavol Dobšinský). See Mrlian, *Štúrovci*, pp. 54ff; Melicherčík, *Pavol Dobšinský*, pp. 39-50.

49 Michal Miloslav Hodža, *Dobruo slovo*, p. 43, claims that the Slav peoples form 'a world nationality,' whereas 'the Magyar nationality will remain for ever merely a local, secondary, small-scale nationality.'

50 He did not mention the Byelorussians or, naturally, the Macedonians.

51 Štúr, *Nárečie slovenské*, pp. 15-20, 24-5, 35-8, 44, 47-8, 53ff, 70-3, 106ff, 125

52 Štúr, *Nauka reči slovenskej*, in *Dielo*, vol. V, pp. 155, 168; *Listy*, vol. I, p. 354. See also Michal Miloslav Hodža, *Epigenes Slovenicus*, p. 16, and *Větín o slovenčině*, p. 14.

53 Štúr, *Starý i nový věk*, pp. 16-18; *Die Beschwerden und Klagen der Slaven*, p. 35; *Dielo*, vol. I, pp. 161-2, 209, 212-16; vol. II, pp. 195, 236, 250-1

54 For the reaction of these Czech liberals, see Pešek, 'The "Czechoslovak" question,' pp. 138-45.

55 Palacký to Kollár, 21 Aug. 1846, in Palacký, 'Dopisy,' p. 480. For Hegel's influence on Štúr see Pražák, 'Hegel bei den Slovaken,' pp. 397ff. In general see Osuský, *Filozofia Štúrovcov* (the three volumes deal respectively with Štúr, Hurban, and Hodža); Chyzhevs'kyi, *Štúrova filozofia života*; Várossova, *Slovenské obrodenecké myslenie*. What I have written above shows that Štúr's idea of Slovak nationality was by no means exclusively a derivative of Hegel's. An attempt was made by Štefan Polakovič (*Začiatky*, esp. chap. 2) – quite unsuccessfully in my opinion – to prove that the nationalism of the *štúrovcy* was mainly the result of Hollý's influence and that 'Czechoslovaks' like Kollár exerted virtually no influence here (cf. Rapant's extremely critical review of Polakovič's book in *Historický sborník*). Studies of the Slovak

national awakening that omit its earliest 'Bernolákite' stage (e.g. Svätopluk Štúr, *Smysel slovenského obrodenia*) appear to me to be equally onesided in the other direction.

56 *Hlasowé*, which appeared in May 1846. I have dealt with it in the previous chapter.

57 Štúr to Hamuljak, 23 June 1846, Štúr, *Listy*, vol. III, p. 50

58 Mráz, 'Z ohlasov,' pp. 26-32. Štúr, though he promised a fuller reply to *Hlasové*, in fact never completed anything beyond newspaper articles. Ctiboh Zoch finished an answer that same year, but censorship prevented its publication until long after his death (*Slovo za slovenčinu*). Hurban reviewed *Hlasové* at length – and with considerable acerbity – in his freshly founded literary journal *Slovenskje pohladi*, vol. I, pt 1 (1846), pp. 35-67; this review was also published as a pamphlet, *Českje hlasi*, and later printed (Podhradsky, *Jozef Miloslav Hurban*) with a tendentious introduction by Juraj Podhradsky depicting Hurban as a Hungarian patriot and rabid Czech-hater. Finally, in 1847 Michal Miloslav Hodža, in *Dobruo slovo*, produced something approaching an official reply from the *štúrovcy*; it was quite broad in scope, not merely refuting the authors of *Hlasové* but also advancing many positive arguments in favour of new Slovak.

59 E.g. Samo Chalupka to S.B. Hroboň, 16 May 1845, in Kleinschnitzová, ed., 'Z dolno-kubínskej pozostalosti,' p. 151

60 *Slovenskje národňje novini*. Vol. IV of the photocopy edition contains the paper's literary supplement, *Orol Tátránski*. The paper ceased publication early in June 1848. For a detailed account of the background to their publication, see Vyvíjalová, *Slovenskje Národňje Novini*.

61 Rapant, 'Štúrove *Slovenskje Národňje Novini*,' p. 9. In May 1842 Štúr had proposed publishing a few articles in *bernoláčina* (see Vyvíjalová, *Slovenskje Národňje Novini*, pp. 66-7).

62 For example, the bookseller, journalist, and publisher Fejérpataky who stood security for it in 1842. For his qualified opposition to *štúrovčina* see his autobiography, *Vlastný životopis*, pp. 71, 72, 75, and his biography by Hučko, *Gašpar Fejérpataky – Belopotocký*, pp. 139-41.

63 Ruttkay, 'O Slovenskýeh národných novinách,' p. 20. For the pre-1848 journalism of Štúr's movement, see Ruttkay, *Prehl'ad dejín*, pp. 188-253, and *Daniel G. Lichard*, pp. 27ff.

64 The literature on these activities (of the kind called in Poland 'organic work') is quite large. In general, see Paučo, *L'udovýchova u štúrovcov*; Rapant, *Slovenské povstanie*, vol. I, pt 1, pp. 145-64; and Pasiar, *Z dejín slovenskej l'udovýchovy*, pp. 53-76. For popular education see Vajcik, 'Štúrovci,' pp. 145-70, and Bakoš, *L'udovít Štúr*. For village libraries see Pasiar, *Dejiny*,

pp. 49-75; for co-operatives see Ruttkay, *Samuel Jurkovič*; for temperance associations see Paučo, *L'udovýchova u štúrovcov*, pp. 105-46.
65 Rapant, ed., *Tatrín*, p. 50
66 Ibid., pp. 32-45. In appendices to his book (nos 11, 12, 16, 18, 19, 27-9, 34-6) Rapant prints the reports (written in Magyar) on Tatrín's activities sent in to the Viceregal Council by the various Hungarian authorities the Council had consulted. Most of them branded Tatrín as a 'panslav' organization and recommended rejection of its application for approval. 'Just as Hungary constitutes one country, so its inhabitants form one nation (Magyarország mint magában egy ország, úgy lakosai egy nemzet)' was a typical response (from the report by the director of the Kassa (Košice) school district, 9 June 1847, ibid., p. 129).
67 Ibid., pp. 11-12. Many documents are printed here from the organization's archives, as well as supplementary materials relating to its history. The choice of the small town of Liptovský Mikuláš for the founding meeting may have been due in part to its symbolic significance in the centre of Slovakia (Ruppeldt, *Koncentračné snahy*, p. 24).
68 Rapant, ed., *Tatrín*, 25-30, 77, 105-7, 147, 148
69 Karol Kuzmány to Tatrín, 14 Oct. 1844, ibid., p. 64.
70 Cited in Žáček, *Čechové a Poláci*, pp. 204-5. Zach was then the agent in Belgrade of the Polish émigré leader Prince Adam Czartoryski.
71 Butvin, *Slovenské národnozjednocovacie hnutie*, pp. 289-93
72 Ibid., p. 345
73 Rapant, ed., *Tatrín*, pp. 30, 144-51. Rapant suggests (p. 6) that the general reluctance of the Slovak Catholic clerical intelligentsia to support Tatrín, despite numerous overtures from the side of Štúr's group, was due to their suspicion of a body that had failed to win legal recognition form the Hungarian authorities.
74 Sources relating to the Catholic clergy who supported Štúr's movement with varying degrees of completeness are fragmentary. See for instance Sedlák, *Ján Andraščík*, pp. 16-20 (cf. p. 31), on a well known Catholic temperance leader; Gajdoš, 'Zabudnutý Štúrov pomocník,' on a Franciscan monk, Anian Dobšovič; Hlušek, 'Z pozostalosti Štefana Holčeka,' pp. 48, 49; Šteller, *Andrej Radlinský*, pp. 11-100, on Radlinský's pre-1848 activities; Viktorín, 'Autobiografia,' p. 133; Martiš, 'Život a dielo Štefana Závodníka,' pp. 19-21, and Paučo, 'Slovakia's mid-nineteenth-century struggle,' pp. 77-8, on another leading Catholic worker for temperance. In general, see Garaj, 'Vzt'ah L'udovíta Štúra.' We may note that some Catholic clergy at this time still supported *bibličtina*.
75 See Rapant, *Slovenský prestolny prosbopis*, vol. II, pp. 237-51, 600-2, for relevant documents.

76 Butvin, 'Jednota,' p. 282
77 For the Union's activities see, in addition to Butvin, ibid., the facsimile edition of the manuscript history by a participant, Dobšinský, *Deje Jednoty*; Pražák, *Literární Levcča*, chaps. 8, 9; and Sedlák, *Strieborný vek*, vol. I, pt 1, vol. II, sections 5, 6 (for eastern Slovakia).
78 Letter from Král', 2 July 1845, in Butvin, 'Jednota,' p. 290. See also pp. 289, 291, and Brtáň, *Život básnika Janka Král'a*, p. 85.
79 Francisci, *Vlastný životopis*, pp. 127-9; Milan Hodža, *Československý rozkol*, pp. 390-7; Arató, *A nemzetiségi kérdés*, vol. II, pp. 146-50, 154-6; Žáček, *Z revolučných ... stykov*, pp. 182-3. Francisci's pamphlet was entitled *Zrkadlo pre l'ud slovenský*. Matula, 'Snahy,' p. 222, distinguishes between what he calls Štúr's 'liberal' and Francisci's 'revolutionary' lines. See also Matula, 'K niektorým otázkam,' pp. 396-406, and 'Slovenska .. ideológia,' pp. 253, 259-61. For Francisci's criticism of Štúr's editorship of the *Slovak National News* as socially too conservative, see Štúr, *Listy*, vol. III, pp. 92-101, 103-4; Sedlák, *Strieborný vek*, vol. II, pp. 324-8.
80 Rapant, 'Vývin slovenskej národnej pospolitosti,' p. 269, and 'Vývin slovenského národného povedomia.'
81 1848 was the year in which the Silesian awakener, Paweł Stalmach, first began to publish in Cieszyn his Polish language weekly, *Tygodnik Cieszyński*. Several Czech writers (e.g. Adamus, 'Štúr a Těšínsko') have argued that Stalmach's rejection of Czech in favour of Polish (from which, it is alleged, stemmed the eventual loss of most of Teschen Silesia to the Poles) was due to Štúr's influence on Stalmach while he was a student at the Bratislava *lycée* in the mid-1840s. In reality, as Stalmach has stated in his autobiography ('Pamiętniki,' pp. 171, 178) he had already made his choice before coming to Bratislava. See also Kudelka, 'Pavel Stalmach,' pp. 47-54, for a refutation of Adamus's thesis. Stalmach in fact was not a linguistic separatist as was Štúr. He wished to integrate his native region with one of its larger neighbours, not to detach it and make it a separate cultural entity.
82 A leaflet written by Hurban and issued in the name of the Slovak National Council in mid-September 1848 described Czechs and Slovaks as forming 'one nation' with 'one language.' It is reprinted in Rapant, *Slovenské povstanie*, vol. II, pt 2, p. 160. Štúr renounced both Czechophilism and Austroslavism a few years later with his book, *Das Slawenthum und die Welt der Zukunft*. It was written in the mid-1850s but published only after his death – in Russian translation, first in 1867 and again in 1909. The original German version was published in Bratislava in 1931 in an edition by J. Jirásek. The author rejects Kollárian cultural slavophilism in favour of a political union of all Slavs under the sceptre of the Russian Tsar. See also Petrovich, 'L'udovít Štúr.'
83 Auty, 'The evolution of literary Slovak,' p. 156

# Bibliography

All places of publication are given in their present-day form. Works appearing after 1973 could not be included.

ADAMOVIČ, ŠTEFAN. *Ján Ladislav Bartholomoeides*. Liptovský Mikuláš, 1942
ADAMUS, A. 'Štúr a Těšínsko.' *Česká Revue* (Prague), XIV (1921), no. 4: 162-5
ARATÓ, ENDRE. *A nemzetiségi kérdés története Magyarországon*. 2 vols. Budapest, 1960
– *Sociálne motívy slovenského národného hnutia v r. 1845-48*. Martin, 1952
AUTY, ROBERT. 'Dialect, *koiné*, and tradition in the formation of literary Slovak.' *Slavonic and East European Review* (London), XXXIX, no. 93 (1961): 339-45
– 'The evolution of literary Slovak,' *Transactions of the Philological Society* (Oxford) (1953): 143-60
– 'Jan Kollár, 1793-1852.' *SEER*, XXXI, no. 76 (1952): 74-91

BAJZA, JOZEF IGNÁC. *René mlád'enca príhodi a skusenost'i*. Ed. Ján Tibenský. Bratislava, 1955
BAKOŠ, L'UDOVÍT. *L'udovít Štúr ako vychovávatel' a bojovník za slovenskú školu*. Bratislava, 1957
BANÍK, ANTON AUGUSTÍN. 'Ján Hollý a slovenské národné obrodenie.' *Vatra* (Ružomberok), VI (1924), no. 1/2: 21-31; no. 3: 57-63; no. 4/5: 91-5
– 'Pomocníci Antona Bernoláka v rokoch 1786-1790 pri diele slovenského literárneho obrodenia.' *Kultúra* (Trnava), IX (1937), no. 9/10: 193-203

– '180 rokov tomu, čo sa narodil vo Veľkých Chlievanoch pri Bánovciach Juraj Palkovič.' *Kultúra,* XV (1943), no. 12: 585-99
BARTEK, HENRICH. *Anton Bernolák.* Trnava, 1937
– 'L. Štúr a slovenčina.' Pp. 291-400 in Ľudovít Štúr, *Nárečie slovenské alebo potreba písania v tomto nárečí.* Ed. H. Bartek. Martin, 1943
BÉDER, JÁN. 'Kollárova koncepcia slovanskej vzájomnosti a *Mladé Slovensko.*' *Historický časopis* (Bratislava), VIII (1960), no. 2/3: 243-7
– 'Nástup generácie *Mladé Slovensko.*' *Slovenská literatúra* (Bratislava), VII (1960), no. 1: 33-52
– 'Pavel Jozef Šafárik a Mladé Slovensko.' *Litteraria* (Bratislava), IV (1961): 267-93
– 'Spoločnosť' česko-slovanská a Slovanský ústav v Bratislave v rokoch 1835–1840.' *Sborník štúdií a prac Vysokej školy pedagogickej v Bratislave (Spoločenské vedy. Slovanský jazyk a literatúra)* (Bratislava), I (1957), no. 1-4(1): 3-80
BERNOLÁK, ANTON. *Bernolákovské polemiky.* Ed. Imrich Kotvan. Bratislava, 1966
– *Gramatické dielo Antona Bernoláka.* Ed. Juraj Pavelek. Bratislava, 1964
'Bernolákismu počiatok a koniec.' *Katolické Noviny* (Trnava), XX (1889), no. 21/22: 172-3
BOBEK, WŁADYSŁAW. 'O historizme Fándlyho.' *Sborník Matice Slovenskej* (Martin), XIV (1936), no. 2: 271-8
BOKES, FRANTIŠEK. *Dejiny Slovákov a Slovenska od najstarších čias až po prítomnosť (Slovenská Vlastiveda,* IV). Bratislava, 1946
– *Vývin predstáv o slovenskom území v 19. storoči.* Martin, 1945
BOTTO, JÚLIUS. *Slováci: Vývin ich národného povedomia.* 3d (one-vol.) ed. Bratislava, 1971
BRTÁŇ, RUDO. 'Slováci a Sreznevskij.' *Slovanský sborník* (Martin), I (1947), no. 3/4: 119-42
– *Štefan Moyses a Chorváti.* Martin, 1949
– *Vznik, vývin a verzie Kollárovej rozpravy o literárnej vzájomnosti.* Liptovský Mikuláš, 1942
– *Život básnika Janka Kráľa,* Martin, 1972
BRTÁŇ, RUDO, ed. 'Z Kollárovej korešpondencie.' *Slovanský sborník,* I (1947), no. 3/4: 218-28
BUJNÁK, PAVOL. *Dr Karol Kuzmány: Život a dielo.* Liptovský Mikuláš, 1927
BUTVIN, JOZEF. 'The Great Moravian Cyril and Methodius tradition in the Slovak national revival.' *Studia historica slovaca* (Bratislava), VII (1972): 96-118
– 'Jednota mládeže slovenskej "Bratstvo slovenskje" (K otázke slovenského

študentského hnutia v r. 1845-1848).' *Sborník filozofickej fakulty Univerzity Komenského* [FFUK] : *Historica* (Bratislava), XV (1964): 279-97
- 'Martin Hamuljak and the fundamental problems of the Slovak national revival.' *Studia historica slovaca,* III (1965): 135-72
- *Slovenské národnozjednocovacie hnutie (1780-1848) (K otázke formovania novodobého slovenského buržoázneho národa).* Bratislava, 1965
- 'Snahy o zakladanie kultúrnych organizácií a spolkov v období slovenského národného obrodenia.' Pp. 21-34 in *Matica slovenská v našich dejinách.* Bratislava, 1963
- 'Tajný politický spolok Vzájomnosť' (1837-1840.' *Sborník FFUK: Historica,* XIV (1963): 3-40

CHALUPKA, JÁN, ed. *Schreiben des Grafen Carl Zay ... an die Professoren zu Leutschau.* Leipzig, 1841
CHOVAN, JURAJ. 'Martin Hamuljak a vývin spisovnej slovenčiny.' *Biografické štúdie* (Martin), I (1970): 17-24
CHOVAN, JURAJ, ed. 'Predhovor k bernolákovmu slováru z roku 1796.' *Literárny Archív 1967* (Martin): 47-92
CHYZHEVS'KYI [ČIŽEVSKIJ], DMYTRO. *Štúrova filozofia života.* Tr. from German. Bratislava, 1941
ČAPEK, JAN B. *Československá literatura toleranční 1781-1861.* 2 vols. Prague, 1933
ČAPEK, THOMAS. *The Slovaks of Hungary: Slavs and Panslavism.* New York, 1906
ČAPLOVIČ [CSAPLOVICS], JÁN. *Gemälde von Ungarn.* 2 vols. Pest, 1829
- *Slawismus und Pseudomagyarismus.* Leipzig, 1842
ČAPLOVIČ, JÁN, ed. *Slowenské wersse.* Pest, 1822 (Reprint, Martin, 1967)
ČECHVALA, MILAN. 'Martin Hamuljak a slovenské národné hnutie v 20-tych až 40-tych rokoch 19. storočia.' *Sborník filozofickej fakulty Univerzity Komenského: Historica* (Bratislava), XVI (1965): 45-76
ČERVENÁK, BENJAMÍN PRAVOSLAV. *Zrcadlo Slowenska.* Pest, 1844

DENIS, ERNEST. *La question d'Autriche: Les Slovaques.* Paris, 1917
DOBROVSKÝ, JOSEF. *Josefa Dobrovského Korrespondence.* Vol. IV, ed. Adolf Patera. Prague, 1913
DOBŠINSKÝ, PAVOL. *Deje Jednoty mládeže slovenskej do roku 1848.* Facsimile ed. Martin, 1972
DOLANSKÝ, JULIUS. 'Česko-slovenská spolupráce v období národního obrození.' Pp. 125-41 in L'udovít Holotík, ed., *O vzájomných vzťahoch Čechov a Slovákov.* Bratislava, 1956

FAITH, ŠTEFAN. 'Slovenskí katolícki kazatelia XVIII storočia.' *Theologica catholica slovaca* (Bratislava), I (1941): 116-38

FÁNDLY, JURAJ. *Výber z diela.* Ed. Ján Tibenský. Bratislava, 1954

FEJÉRPATAKY-BELOPOTOCKÝ, GAŠPAR. *Vlastný životopis (Po rok 1850).* Liptovský Mikuláš, 1926

FERIENČIKOVA, ANNA, ed. *Knižnica Slovanského ústavu v Bratislave.* Bratislava, 1972

FRANCISCI, JÁN. *Vlastný životopis.* Bratislava, 1956

FRANTSEV [FRANCEV], V.A. *Cheshsko-slovenskii raskol i ego otgoloski v literature sorokovykh godov.* Warsaw, 1915

– 'Štúrovo "schisma" a jeho ohlasy.' *Časopis pro moderní filologii a literatury* (Prague), IV (1914), no. 2: 97-105; no. 3: 201-12


GAJDOŠ, VŠEVLAD J. 'Zabudnutý Štúrov pomocník,' *Kultúra* (Trnava), vol. XVI (1944), no. 2: 78-84

GARAJ, JÁN. 'Vzt'ah L'udovíta Štúra k bernolákovcom.' *Slovenská reč* (Bratislava), XXI (1956), no. 3/4: 207-18

*Gitřenka, čili výborněgšj práce učenců Česko-Slowenských A.W. Lewočských.* Levoča, 1840

GLASSL, HORST. *Die slovakische Geschichtswissenschaft nach 1945.* Wiesbaden, 1971

GOGOLÁK, LAJOS [LUDWIG VON]. *Beiträge zur Geschichte des slowakischen Volkes.* Munich, Vol. I: *Die Nationswerdung der Slowaken und die Anfänge der tschechoslowakischen Frage (1526-1790).* 1963. Vol. II: *Die slowakische nationale Frage in der Reformepoche Ungarns (1790-1848).* 1969. Vol. III: *Zwischen zwei Revolutionen (1848-1919).* 1972

– 'Die historische Entwicklung des slowakischen Nationalbewusstseins.' Pp. 27-116 in *Die Slowakei als mitteleuropaisches Problem in Geschichte und Gegenwart.* Munich, 1965

– *Pánszlávizmus.* Budapest, 1940

– 'A szlovák és ruszin nemzetiség története.' Pp. 253-78 in Gyula Szekfű, ed., *A magyarság és a szlávok.* Budapest, 1942

GOLÁN, KAROL. *Štúrovské pokolenie (Výber z diela).* Bratislava, 1964


HABOVŠTIAKOVÁ, KATARÍNA. *Bernolákovo jazykovedné dielo.* Bratislava, 1968

HAMULJAK, MARTIN. *Listy Martina Hamuljaka.* Vol. I, ed. Augustín Mat'ovčík. Martin, 1969

HANÁK, J. 'Slovaks and Czechs in the early 19th century.' *Slavonic (and East European) Review* (London), X, no. 30 (1932): 588-601

HANUŠ, JOSEF. *Dobrovský a Slovensko. Sborník filosofické fakulty University Komenského v Bratislavě*, II, no. 23 [6]. Bratislava, 1924
HARAKSIM, L. 'Od Kollárova slovanství k slovenství (1835-1848).' Pp. 158-67 in Vladislav Št'astný et al., eds, *Slovanství v národním životě Čechů a Slováků*. Prague, 1968
HELCELET, JAN. *Korrespondence a zápisky Jana Helceleta*. Ed. Jan Kabelík, 1910
HENDRICH, JOSEF. *'Hlasové o potřebě jednoty spisovného jazyka.' Bratislava* (Bratislava), IV (1930): 371-84
HIRNER, ALEXANDER. *Ján Feješ: Jeho dielo a myšlienková sústava*. Martin, 1942
*Hlasowé o potřebě jednoty spisowného jazyka pro Čechy, Morawany a Slowáky.* Prague, 1846
HLUŠEK, ŠTEFAN. 'Z pozostalosti Štefana Holčeka.' *Sborník literárno-vedeckého odboru Spolka Sv. Vojtecha* (Trnava), II, no. 1 (1935): 41-98
HODŽA, MICHAL MILOSLAV. *Dubruo slovo Slovákom súcim na slovo*. Facsimile reprint. Bratislava, 1970
- *Epigenes Slovenicus*. Levoča, 1847
- *Der Slowak. Beiträge zur Beleuchtung der slawischen Frage in Ungarn.* Prague, 1848
- *Větín o slovenčině*. Levoča, 1848
HODŽA, MILAN. *Československý rozkol: Príspevky k dejinám slovenčiny*. Martin, 1920
HOIČ, SAMUEL. *Apologie des ungrischen Slawismus*. Leipzig, 1843
- *Sollen wir Magyaren werden?* Karlovac, 1833
HOLLÝ, JÁN. *Básně*. 4 vols. Buda, 1841-2
- *Korešpondencia Jána Hollého*. Ed. Jozef Ambruš. Martin, 1967
HOLOTÍK, L'UDOVÍT, ed. *L'udovit Štúr und die slawische Wechselseitigkeit.* Bratislava, 1969
HOLOTÍK, L'UDOVÍT, et al., eds. *Dejiny Slovenska*, Bratislava. I (1961); II (1968)
HROCH, MIROSLAV. *Die Vorkämpfer der nationalen Bewegung bei den kleinen Völkern Europas: Eine vergleichende Analyse zur gesellschaftlichen Schichtung der patriotischen Gruppen*. Prague, 1968
*Hronka* (Banská Bystrica). 3 vols. 1836-8
HUČKO, JÁN. *Gašpar Fejérpataky-Belopotocký (Život a dielo)*. Bratislava, 1965
- *Michal Miloslav Hodža*. Bratislava, 1970
HURBAN, JOZEF MILOSLAV. *Cesta Slováka k slovenským bratom na Morave a v Čechách 1839*. Bratislava, 1960
- *Českje hlasi prot'i slovenčiňe*. Skalica, 1846
- 'Dva listy Miloslava Jozefa Hurbana.' Ed. Jaroslav Vlček and Flora Kleinschnitzová. *Sborník Matice Slovenskej* (Martin), I (1922), no. 5/6: 87-94

– *L'udovít Štúr.* Ed. Jozef Štolc. Bratislava, 1959
– *Slovensko a jeho život literárny.* Ed. Rudolf Chmel. Bratislava, 1972
– *Slovo o spolkách mjernost'i a školách ňedélních.* Banská Bystrica, 1846
– *Unia, čili spojení Lutheranů s Kalvíny v Uhrách.* Buda, 1846
HÝSEK, MILOSLAV. 'Dějiny t. zv. moravského separatismu.' *Časopis Matice moravské* (Brno), XXXIII (1909): 24-51, 146-72

JANKOVIČ, VENDELÍN. *Ján Čaplovič: Život, osobnost', dielo.* Martin, 1945
JÓNA, EUGEN. 'Účast' L'udovíta Štúra pri utváraní spisovnej slovenčiny.' *Slovenská reč* (Bratislava), XXI (1956), no. 3/4: 131-46
– 'Účast' M.M. Hodžu pri formovaní spisovnej slovenčiny.' *Slovenská reč,* XXXV (1970), no. 2: 65-8; no. 3: 134-41; no. 4: 199-205
*Jitřenka,* see *Gitřenka.*

KIMBALL, STANLEY B. *The Austro-Slav Revival: A Study of Nineteenth-Century Literary Foundations.* Transactions of the American Philosophical Society, NS, LXIII, pt 4. Philadelphia, 1973
KIRSCHBAUM, J.M. *Anton Bernolák: The First Codifier of the Slovak Language (1762-1813).* Winnipeg and Cleveland, 1962
– *L'udovít Štúr and His Place in the Slavic World.* Winnipeg and Cleveland, 1958
– *Pan-Slavism in Slovak Literature: Ján Kollár–Slovak Poet of Panslavism (1793-1852).* Winnipeg and Toronto, 1966
– *Pavel Jozef Šafárik and his Contribution to Slavic Studies.* Cleveland and Winnipeg, 1962
KLATÍK, ZLATKO. 'Ilýrske hnutie a spisovná slovenčina.' *Slovenská reč* (Bratislava), XXVIII (1963), no. 5: 257-68
KLEINSCHNITZOVÁ, FLORA. *Andrej Sládkovič a jeho doba (1820-1850).* Prague, 1928
KLEINSCHNITZOVÁ, FLORA, ed. 'Z dolno-kubínskej pozostalosti Sama Bohdana Hroboňa.' *Sborník Matice Slovenskej* (Martin), V (1927), no. 3/4: 122-55
KOHN, HANS. *Pan-Slavism: Its History and Ideology.* Rev. ed. New York, 1960
KOHUTH, JOSEF. 'Jos. Ign. Bajza a slovenské prebudenie.' *Tovaryšstvo* (Ružomberok), II (1895): 15-22
– 'Učené slovenské tovaryšstvo.' *Tovaryšstvo,* I (1893): 25-50
KOLLÁR, JAN. 'Cestopis obsahující cestu do horní Italie ... roku 1841 konanou a sepsanou' [1843]. In *Spisy Jana Kollára.* Vol. III. Prague, 1862
– 'Myšlénky o libozwučnosti řečj wůbec, obzwlaště českoslowanské.' *Krok* (Prague), I, no. 3 (1822): 32-47

– *Národnie spievanky.* 2 vols. Bratislava, 1953
– *Nedělnj, swátečné i přjležitostné kázně a řeči.* Vol. I; Pest, 1831. Vol. II;
Buda, 1844
– 'Některé listy z korrespondence Jana Kollára v letech 1816-1851.' *Časopis Musea království českého* (Prague), LXVII (1893), 177-211
– 'Paměti z mladších let života.' In *Spisy Jana Kollára.* Vol. IV. Prague, 1863
– with P.J. Šafařík. *Pjsně swětské lidu slowenského w Uhřjch.* Vol. I; Pest, 1823.
Vol. II (entitled *Pjsně swětské lidu slawenského w Uhrách*); Pest, 1827
– *Rozpravy o slovanské vzájemnosti.* Ed. Miloš Weingart. Prague, 1929
– 'Vzájemné dopisy Václava Hanky a Jana Kollára.' *Časopis Musea království českého,* LXXI (1897): 227-45
KOTVAN, IMRICH. *Bernolákovci.* Trnava, 1948
– *Juraj Fándly (1750-1811).* Trnava, 1946
KOTVAN, IMRICH. ed. *Bibliografia Bernolákovcov.* Martin, 1957
*K počiatkom slovenského národného obrodenia.* Bratislava, 1964
KRAUS, CYRIL. 'Kuzmány a Štúrovci.' Pp. 108-19, in *Karol Kuzmány (1806-1866).* Martin, 1967
KRČMÉRY, ŠTEFAN. 'Prielom Sama Chalupku do spisovnej slovenčiny roku 1832.' *Slovenské pohl'ady,* (Martin), XLVII (1931), no. 3: 175-89
– 'Prielom štúrovských básnikov do spisovnej slovenčiny pod zorným uhlom Chalupkovho prielomu z roku 1832.' *Slovenské pohl'ady* (Martin), XLVIII (1932), no. 4: 245-55
KUDĚLKA, MILAN. 'Pavel Stalmach a Slovensko.' *Slezský sborník* (Opava), L (1952), no. 1: 25-54
KÚTNIK ŠMÁLOV, JOZEF. *Zástoj katolíckej hierarchie v slovenskom národnom a kultúrnom živote.* Ružomberok, 1948
*Kwěty* (Prague), 14 vols. 1834-47

LANŠTJÁK, O.H. *Šturowčina a posauzení knihy 'Nárečja Slowenskuo.'* Buda, 1847
LAUNER, ŠTEPAN. *Povaha slovanstva se zvláštním ohleden na spisovní řeč Čechů, Moravanů, Slezáků a Slováků.* Leipzig, 1847
– *Slowo k národu swému.* Banská Štiavnica, 1847
LAZAR, ERVÍN. *Jonáš Záborský: Život–Literárne dielo–Korešpondencia.* Bratislava, 1956
LEHOCKA, J.M. 'Listy Johany Miloslavy Lehockej Bohuslave Rajskej a Samoslavovi Bohdanovi Hroboňovi.' Ed. Eugen Klementis. *Literárny archiv (Pramene a dokumenty) 1970* (Martin), (1971): 143-69
LOCHER, THEODOR JAKOB GOTTLIEB. *Die nationale Differenzierung und Integrierung der Slovaken und Tschechen in ihrem geschichtlichen Verlauf bis 1848.* Haarlem, 1931

- 'Het Panslavisme bij de Tsjechen en Slovaken.' Pp. 146-59 in his *Geschiedenis van ver en nabij.* Leiden, 1970

*L'udovít Štúr: Život a dielo 1815-1856.* Bratislava, 1956

MARTÁK, JÁN. 'Poézia levočskej Pamätnice a Jitřenky.' *Literárny archiv* (Martin), IX (1972 [1973]): 47-83

- *Útok na spisovnú slovenčinu roku 1847/48 a jeho ciel'.* Martin, 1938

MARTIŠ, JÁN. 'Život a dielo Štefana Závodníka.' *Biografické štúdie* (Martin), IV (1973): 11-37

MAT'OVČÍK, AUGUSTÍN. *Martin Hamuljak (1789-1859): Život, dielo, osobnost'.* Bratislava, 1971

- 'Príspevok k životu a dielu Jána Herkel'a.' *Historické štúdie* (Bratislava), IX (1964): 5-27

MATULA, VLADIMÍR. 'Bogoslav Šulek a Mladé Slovensko.' *Historické štúdie* (Bratislava), XIII (1968): 201-25

- 'K niektorým otázkam slovenského národného hnutia štyridsiatych rokov XIX. stor.' *Historický časopis* (Bratislava), II (1954), no. 3: 375-406

- *L'udovít Štúr (1815-1856).* Bratislava, 1956

- 'Mladé Slovensko a Juhoslovania.' Pp. 106-33 in Jozef Hrozienčik, ed., *Československo a Juhoslávia: Z dejín československo-juhoslovanských vzt'ahov.* Bratislava, 1968

- 'Slovanska vzájomnost-národooslobodzovacia ideológia slovenského národného hnutia (1835-1849).' *Historický časopis* (Bratislava), VIII (1960), no. 2/3: 248-64

- 'Snahy o prehl'benie demokratickej línie *Slovenských národných novín* a formulovanie revolučného programu slovenského národného hnutia (1845-1848).' *Historický časopis* (Bratislava), VI (1958), no. 2: 202-23

MELICHERČÍK, ANDREJ. *Pavol Dobšinský: Portrét života a diela.* Bratislava, 1959

MENČÍK, FERDINAND. *Jiří Ribay. Kapitola z dějin literárních.* Vienna, 1892

MINÁRIK, JOZEF. 'Pavel Jozef Šafárik a slovenská literatúra.' *Litteraria* (Bratislava), IV (1961): 183-205

MIŠKOVIČ, ALOJZ. 'Tablic češtil!?' *Kultúra* (Trnava), VIII (1936), no. 4: 163-7

MRÁZ, ANDREJ. *Dejiny slovenskej literatúry.* In *Slovenská vlastiveda,* V, pt 1. Bratislava, 1948

- *L'udovít Štúr.* Bratislava, 1948

- 'Zástoj cyrilometodejskej idey u bernolákovcov.' *Sborník filozofickej fakulty Univerzity Komenského* [FFUK]: *Philologica* (Bratislava), XIV (1962): 7-53

- 'Z ohlasov na československé vzt'ahy v štúrových Slovenských Národných Novinách a Orle Tatránskom.' *Sborník FFUK: Philologica,* XIII (1961): 3-43

MRLIAN, ONDREJ. *Jozef Miloslav Hurban.* Martin, 1959

MRLIAN, RUDOLF. *Štúrovci a ústna slovesnost' (Funkcia folkloru u štúrovcov).* Liptovský Mikuláš, 1943

*Ňitra* (Bratislava), II (1844)

NOVOTNÝ, JAN. *Češi a Slováci za národního obrození a do vzniku československého státu.* Prague, 1968

– 'Ke krizi čechoslovakismu a ilyrismu v mezislovanských vztazích v předvečer revoluce 1848.' Pp. 134-45 in Jozef Hrozienčik, ed., *Československo a Juhoslávia: Z dejín československo-juhoslovanských vzt'ahov.* Bratislava, 1968

– 'Ke vzájemnému vztahu Pavla Josefa Šafaříka se Šturovci.' Pp. 41-56 in *Odkaz P.J. Šafárika. Slovanské štúdie,* VI. Bratislava, 1963

*O bratrské družbě Čechů a Slováků za národního obrození.* Prague, 1959

OBERUČ, JÁN. 'Črty z dejín evanj. a. v. cirkvi na Slovensku v prvej polovici 19. storočia.' Pp. 29-47 in J. Oberuč, ed., *Sborník zpěvníka evanjelického 1842– 1942.* Liptovský Mikuláš, 1942

ORMIS, JÁN V. *Bibliografia Jána Kollára.* Bratislava, 1954

– *Bibliografia L'udovíta Štúra.* Martin, 1958

– *O reč a národ: Slovenské národné obrany z rokov 1832-1848,* Bratislava, 1973

– 'Slovenské národné obrany v rokoch 1832-1848.' *Historický časopis* (Bratislava), XI (1963), no. 4: 552-79

ORMIS, JÁN V., ed. *Súčasníci o L'udovítovi Štúrovi.* Bratislava, 1955

*Orol Tatránski* (Bratislava), 1845-8. Reprint, 1956. Vol. IV of *Slovenskje národňje novini.*

OSUSKÝ, SAMUEL ŠTEFAN. *Filozofia Šturovcov.* 3 vols (Myjava). I: *Šturova filozofia.* 1926. 2d ed., Bratislava, 1936. II: *Hurbanova filozofia.* 1928. III: *Hodžova filozofia.* 1932

PALACKÝ, FRANTIŠEK. 'Dopisy Františka Palackého Janu Kollárovi.' Ed. A.J. Vrt'átko, *Časopis Musea království českého* (Prague), Vol. LIII (1879): 378-97 (pt 1), 467-81 (pt 2)

– *Františka Palackého Korrespondence a Zápisky.* Ed. V.J. Nováček. Vol. II. Prague, 1902

– with P.J. Šafařík. *Počátkové českého básnictví obzvláště prozódie.* Bratislava, 1961

PALKOVIČ, JIŘÍ. *Böhmisch-deutsch-lateinisches Wörterbuch, mit Beyfügung der den Slowaken und Mähren eigenen Ausdrücke und Redensarten ...* Vol. I; Prague, 1820. Vol. II; Bratislava, 1821

- 'Pogednánj o Slowácých a zwlásstě gegich řeči.' *Týdennjk, aneb Cýsařské královské národnj nowiny* (Bratislava), VI (1817), no. 11 (21 March): 173-80; no. 12 (28 March): 189-96
- 'Předmluwa.' *Týdennjk*, I (1812): iii-xx
PALKOVIČ, KONŠTANTÍN. 'Ctiboh Zoch ako jazykovedec.' *Slovenská reč* (Bratislava), XXX (1965), no. 6: 321-30
PASIAR, ŠTEFAN. *Dejiny slovenských ľudových knižníc.* Martin, 1957
- *Z dejín slovenskej ľudovýchovy do roku 1918.* Martin, 1952
PASTRNEK, FRANTIŠEK, ed. *Jan Kollár 1793-1852: Sborník statí ...* Vienna, 1893
PAUČO, JOZEF [JOSEPH]. *Ľudovýchova u štúrovcov: Obdobie 'Slovenských národných novín.'* Martin, 1943
- 'Slovakia's mid-nineteenth-century struggle for national life.' *Slovak Studies* (Rome), I (1961): 69-83
PAUL, KAREL. *Pavel Josef Šafařík: Život a dílo.* Prague, 1961
PAULINY, EUGEN. 'Čeština a jej význam pri rozvoji slovenského spisovného jazyka a našej národnej kúltury.' Pp. 99-124 in Ľudovít Holotík, ed., *O vzájomných vzťahoch Čechov a Slovákov.* Bratislava, 1956
- *Dejiny spisovnej slovenčiny.* In *Slovenská vlastiveda.* Vol. V, pt 1. Bratislava, 1948
PEŠEK, THOMAS G. 'The "Czechoslovak" question on the eve of the 1848 revolution.' Pp. 131-45 in Peter Brock and H. Gordon Skilling, eds, *The Czech Renascence of the Nineteenth Century: Essays presented to Otakar Odložilík in honour of his seventieth birthday.* Toronto, 1970
PETROVICH, MICHAEL B. 'Ľudovít Štúr and Russian panslavism.' *Journal of Central European Affairs* (Boulder, Colo.), XII (1952), no. 1: 1-19
PEUKERT, HERBERT. *Die Slawen der Donaumonarchie und die Universität Jena 1700-1848.* Berlin, 1958
PIŠÚT, MILAN. *Literárne štúdie a portrety: Z novšej slovenskej a českej literatúry.* Bratislava, 1955
- *Počiatky básnickej školy Štúrovej.* Bratislava, 1938
- with Karol Rosenbaum and Viktor Kochol. *Literatúra národného obrodenia.* Vol. II of *Dejiny slovenskej literatúry.* Bratislava, 1960
*Plody zboru učenců řeči československané prešperského.* Bratislava, 1836
PODHRADSKY, JURAJ, ed. *Jozef Miloslav Hurban a jeho borba proti Čechom a Čechoslovákom v časopise 'Slovenskje Pohladi' r. 1846.* Budapest, 1922
POLAKOVIČ, ŠTEFAN. *Začiatky slovenskej národnej filozofie.* Bratislava, 1944
PRAŽÁK, ALBERT. *Dějiny spisovná slovenštiny po dobu štúrovu.* Prague, 1922
- 'Hegel bei den Slovaken.' Pp. 397-429 in D. Chyzhevs'kyi, ed., *Hegel bei den Slaven.* Liberec, 1934

- 'Kollárova myšlenka slovanské vzájemnosti a Slováci.' Pp. 298-338 in Jiří Horák, ed., *Slovanská vzájemnost 1836-1936*. Prague, 1938
- *Literárni Levoča: Příspěvky k některým epísodám jejího vývoje*. Prague, [1939]
- *Obrozenská Bratislava*. Bratislava, 1928
- 'The Slovak sources of Kollár's Pan-Slavism.' *Slavonic and East European Review* (London), VI, no. 18 (1928): 579-92
- *Slovenská otázka v době J.M. Hurbana*. Sborník filozofické fakulty University Komenského v Bratislavě. [FFUK], I, no. 13. Bratislava, 1923
- *Slovenské studie*. Sborník FFUK, IV, no. 43. Bratislava, 1926

RAPANT, DANIEL. 'Bélovo mad'arónstvo.' *Prúdy* (Bratislava), XII (1928), no. 4: 171-81
- 'Doba štúrovská (O jej štúdiu).' *Historický sborník: Časopis historického odboru MS* (Martin), IV (1946), no. 2: 129-36
- *K počiatkom mad'arizácie*. 2 vols. Bratislava, 1927-31
- 'K pokusom o novú historicko-filozofickú koncepciu slovenského národného obrodenia.' *Slovenská Literatúra* (Bratislava), XII (1965), no. 5: 493-506
- *Mad'arónstvo Bernolákovo*. Bratislava, 1930. Reprinted from *Slovenské dielo*, 1929-30
- 'Nastolenie spisovnej slovenčiny.' *Služba* (Bratislava), VIII (1944), no. 1/2: 16-28
- 'Predzpěvníkové polstoročie (1792-1842).' Pp. 7-13 in Ján Oberuč, ed., *Sborník zpěvníka evanjelického 1842-1942*. Liptovský Mikuláš, 1942
- review of Š. Polakovič, *Začiatky slovenskej národnej filozofie*. In *Historický sborník* (Martin), III (1945), no. 1-4: 330-5
- *Sedliacke povstanie na východnom Slovensku roku 1831*. 2 vols in 3. Bratislava, 1953
- *Slovenské povstanie roku 1848-49: Dejiny a dokumenty*. Vol. I, pt 1; Martin, 1937. Vol. V, pt 1; Bratislava, 1967
- *Slovenský prestolny prosbopis z roku 1842*. 2 vols. Liptovský Mikuláš, 1943
- 'Štúrovci a Slovanstvo.' *Slovanský sborník* (Martin), I (1947), no. 1/2: 22-34
- 'Štúrove "Slovenskje Národňje Novini": Zápas o ich povolenie.' *Elán* (Prague), IX (1939), no. 7/8: 8, 9
- 'Vývin slovenského národného povedomia.' *Historický sborník* (Martin), V (1947), no. 1: 1-16
- 'Vývin slovenskej národnej pospolitosti.' *Historický sborník* (Martin), IV (1946), no. 3/4: 257-74

RAPANT, DANIEL, ed. *Ilegálna mad'arizácia 1790-1840*. Martin, 1947

– *Tatrín (Osudy a zápasy)*. Martin, 1950
REKEM, JOHN [JÁN]. *Slovak Literature and National Consciousness before Anton Bernolák (1762-1813)*. Cleveland, 1964
ROSENBAUM, KAROL. *Pavel Jozef Šafárik*. Bratislava, 1961
– *Poézia národného obrodenia (Koncepcie a dielo)*. Bratislava, 1970
– 'Vzt'ah Karola Kuzmányho k literatúre národného obrodenia.' Pp. 54-67 in *Karol Kuzmány (1806-1866)*. Martin, 1967
RUPPELDT, FEDOR. *Koncentračné snahy slovenské do roku 1918*. Martin, 1928
RUTTKAY, FRAŇO. *Daniel G. Lichard a slovenské novinárstvo jeho doby*. Martin, 1961
– 'O Slovenských národných novinách.' Pamphlet inserted in 1956 reprint of *Slovenskje národňje novini*
– *Prehl'ad dejín slovenského novinárstva do roku 1861*. Bratislava, 1961
– *Samuel Jurkovič: Priekopník slovenského družstevníctva a jeho doba*. 2d rev. ed. Bratislava, 1965

SCHULEK, TIBÈRE [TIBOR]. 'Une famille de Haute-Hongrie au XIX$^e$ siècle.' *Revue d'histoire comparée* (Paris), XXII [NS II] (1944): 139-44
SEDLÁK, IMRICH. *Ján Andraščík*. Košice, 1965
– *Strieborný vek: Národno-kultúrny a literárny pohyb na východnom Slovensku v období národného obrodenia*. 2 vols. Košice, 1970
SEMIAN, MICHAL. *Kratické hystorycké vypsánj knižat a králů uherských ... w slovenském gazyku*. Bratislava, 1786
SETON-WATSON, R.W. *Racial Problems in Hungary*. London, 1908
*Slovenskje národňje novini* (Bratislava), 1845-8. Reprint, 4 vols in 3. 1956
*Slovenskje pohladi na vedi, umeňja a literatúra* (Skalica), I (1846-7)
SOJKOVÁ, ZDENKA. *Skvitne ešte život: Kniha o L'udovítovi Štúrovi*. Tr. from Czech by Július Molitoris. Bratislava, 1965
STALMACH, PAWEŁ. 'Pamiętniki Pawła Stalmacha.' In E. Grim, *Paweł Stalmach. Jego życie i działalność w świetle prawdy*. Cieszyn, 1910
STANISLAV, JÁN. *Z rusko-slovenských kultúrnych stykov v časoch Jána Hollého a L'udovíta Štúra*. Bratislava, 1957
*Staré nowiny liternjho uměni* (Banská Bystrica). May 1785–April 1786
SZABÓ, ZOLTAN. 'A cseh-tót szellemi közösség kezdetei. Ribay György életműve.' *Archivum philologicum: Egyetemes philologiai közlöny* (Budapest), LXI (1937), no. 4-9: 169-207
SZEKFŰ, JULES [GYULA]. *État et nation*. Paris, 1945
SZEKFŰ, GYULA, ed. *Iratok a magyar államnyelv kérdésének történetéhez 1790-1848*. Budapest, 1926

SZIKLAY, LÁSZLÓ. *Launer István: Egy 1848. évi szlovák röpirat szerzője.* Budapest, 1948
- 'Mad'arské vzt'ahy Jána Kollára v Pešti.' Pp. 85-121 in *Dějiny a národy: Literárněhistorické studie o československo-mad'arských vztazích.* Prague, 1965

ŠAFAŘÍK, PAVEL JOSEF. 'Dopisy Pavla Jos. Šafaříka Janu Kollárovi.' *Časopis Musea království českého* (Prague), XLVII (1873): 119-47, 382-407; XLVIII (1874): 54-90, 278-99, 414-26; XLIX (1875): 134-52
- *Geschichte der slawischen Sprache und Literatur nach allen Mundarten.* 2d ed. Prague, 1869
- *Korespondence Pavla Josefa Šafaříka.* Ed. V.A. Francev [Frantsev]. 2 vols. Prague, 1927-8 [Cited as *Korespondence*]
- *Korespondence Pavla Josefa Šafaříka s Františkem Palackým.* Ed. Věnceslava Bechyňová and Zoe Hauptová. Prague, 1961 [Cited as *Korespondence s Palackým*]
- *Listy Pavla Jozefa Šafárika Martinovi Hamuljakovi.* Ed. Augustín Mat'ovčík. Martin, 1965
- *Slovanský národopis.* 4th ed. Ed. Hana Hynková et al. Prague, 1955
- *Slowanské starožitnosti.* Prague, 1837
- See Kollár, *Pjsně.*
- See Palacký, *Počátkové.*

ŠKULTÉTY, JOZEF [JOSEPH]. 'D'ord' Kossuth.' *Slovenské pohl'ady* (Martin), I (1881), no. 6: 549-55
- 'Kto sostavil prvý sväzok Pjsní swetských lidu slowenského w Uhřjch.' *Slovenské pohl'ady,* XVII (1897), no. 5: 316-19
- *Sketches from Slovak History.* Middletown Pa., 1930
- '*Stare Noviny* – Bernolák.' *Slovenské pohl'ady,* XVII (1897), no. 9: 552-7
- *Sto dvadsat'pät rokov zo slovenského života 1790-1914.* 2d rev. ed. Martin, 1920

ŠKULTÉTY, JOZEF, ed. 'Slovenské piesne Sama Chalupku do 1834.' *Slovenské pohl'ady,* XVII (1897), no. 2: 125-8

ŠTEFÁNEK, ANTON. 'Kollárov nacionalismus (Homoetnologická štúdia).' Pp. 339-89 in Jiří Horák, ed., *Slovanská vzájemnost 1836-1936.* Prague, 1938
- 'Osvietenstvo na Slovensku.' *Bratislava* (Bratislava), IV (1930): 13-24

ŠTELLER, FERDINAND. *Andrej Radlinský: Jeho život z boj za práva národa slovenského.* 2 vols in 1. Trnava, 1934

ŠTÚR, L'UDOVÍT. *Die Beschwerden und Klagen der Slaven in Ungarn über die gesetzwidrigen Uebergriffe der Magyaren.* Leipzig, 1843

– *Dielo v piatich zväzkoch.* Bratislava, Vol. I, 1954. Vol. II, 1956. Vol. V, 1957
– *Listy L'udovíta Štúra.* Ed. Jozef Ambruš. 3 vols. Bratislava, 1954-60
– *Nárečie slovenské alebo potreba písania v tomto náreci.* Ed. Henrich Bartek.
  Martin, 1973
– *Das neunzehnte Jahrhundert und der Magyarismus.* Vienna, 1845
– *Das Slawenthum und die Welt der Zukunft.* Ed. Josef Jirásek. Bratislava, 1931
– *Starý i nový věk Slováků.* Ed. Josef Jirásek. Bratislava, 1935
ŠTÚR, SVÄTOPLUK. *Smysel slovenského obrodenia.* Liptovský Mikuláš, 1948
ŠUHAJDA, L.M. *Der magyarismus in Ungarn in rechtlicher, geschichtlicher und*
  *sprachlicher Hinsicht* ... Leipzig, 1834


TABLIC, BOHUSLAV. *Poezye.* 4 vols. Vác, 1806-12
TABLIC, BOHUSLAV, ed. *Slowensstj werssowcy.* Vol. I; Skalica, 1805. Vol. II;
  Vác, 1809
*Tatranka* (Bratislava). 3 vols. 1832-46
THUN, LEO VON. *Die Stellung der Slowaken in Ungarn.* Prague, 1843
TIBENSKÝ, JÁN. 'Bernolák's influence and the origins of the Slovak awakening.'
  *Studia historica slovaca* (Bratislava), II (1964): 140-89
– 'Formovanie sa ideológie slovenskej feudálnej národnosti a buržuázneho národa.'
  *Historický časopis* (Bratislava), XIX (1971), no. 4: 575-91
– 'The function of the Cyril and Methodius and the Great Moravian traditions in
  the ideology of the Slovak feudal nationality.' *Studia historica slovaca,* VII
  (1972): 69-95
– 'Ideológia slovenskej feudálnej národnosti pred národným obrodením.' Pp. 92–
  113 in *Slováci a ich národný vývin.* Bratislava, 1966
– *J. Papánek – J. Sklenár: Obrancovia slovenskej národnosti v XVIII. storoči.*
  Martin, 1958
– 'K starším i novším názorom na A. Bernoláka, bernolákovské hnutie a slovenské
  národné obrodenie.' *Historický časopis,* XIV (1966), no. 3: 329-71
– 'Počiatky slovenského národného obrodenia.' *Historický časopis,* II (1954),
  no. 4: 520-38
– 'Vznik, vývoj a význam vel'komoravskej tradície v slovenskem národnom
  obrodení.' Pp. 142-53 in L'udovít Holotík, ed., *O vzájomných vzt'ahoch*
  *Čechov a Slovákov.* Bratislava, 1956
TIBENSKÝ, JÁN, ed. *Chvály a obrany slovenského národa.* Bratislava, 1965
TKADLEČKOVÁ-VANTUCHOVÁ, JARMILA. *Češi a Slováci v národooslobodzovacom*
  *boji do rakúsko-uhorského vyrovnania roku 1867.* Bratislava, 1970
TÓBIK, ŠTEFAN. 'Pavel Jozef Šafárik a slovenské nárečia.' Pp. 223-34 in *Odkaz*
  *P.J. Šafárika. Slovanské štúdie,* VI. Bratislava, 1963
– *Šafárikov a Kollárov jazyk.* Bratislava, 1966

TOMÁŠIK, SAMO. 'Listy Sama Tomášika Augustovi Horislavovi Škultétymu.'
Ed. Bedřich Heckel. *Literárny archiv* (Martin), IX (1972): 7-45
- 'Vlastný životopis.' *Slovenské poľady* (Martin), XXI (1901), no. 4: 204-11
TOURTZER [TURCEROVÁ], HELENA. *Louis Štúr et l'idée de l'indépendance slovaque (1815-1856)*. Cahors and Alençon, 1913
TURCEROVÁ, HELENA. 'Styky slavianofilov so Slovákmi a ich vplyv na odtrhnutie sa Slovákov od Čechov.' *Prúdy* (Ružomberok), IV (1913), no. 9: 345-50

ÚRHEGYI, EMILIA. 'Bernolák Antal jelentősége a tót művelődés történetében.'
Pp. 457-74 in *Emlékkönyv Melich János hetvenedik születésenapjára*.
Budapest, 1942
- 'Un chapitre de l'histoire du langage littéraire slovaque (Antoine Bernolák: sa vie et sa mission).' *Revue d'histoire comparée* (Budapest and Paris), XXI [NS I, no. 1-2] (1943): 167-92

VAJCIK, PETER. 'Štúrovci a boj o slovenskú školu.' *Pedagogický sborník* (Martin), IX (1942), no. 4/5: 145-70
VÁROSSOVÁ, ELENA. *Slovenské obrodenecké myslenie*. Bratislava, 1963
*Veľká Morava a naša doba*. Bratislava, 1963
VIKTORÍN, JOZEF K. 'Autobiografia Jozefa K. Viktorína.' Ed. Anton Aug. Baník.
*Sborník literárno-vedeckého odboru Spolku Sv. Vojtecha* (Trnava), II, no. 1 (1935): 99-167
- 'Ján Kalinčák. Obrázok životopisný.' *Lipa* (Pest), II (1862): 99-130
VILIKOVSKÝ, JAN. *Dějiny literárních společností malohontských*.
Bratislava, 1935
VLČEK, JAROSLAV. *Dejiny literatúry slovenskej*. 4th ed. Bratislava, 1953
- *Kapitoly zo slovenskej literatury*. Bratislava, 1954
- 'Kterak Šafařík smýšlel o literární jednotě československé.' *Časopis Matice Moravské* (Brno), XIX (1895): 293-306
- *Slovensku*. Martin, 1932
VOLF, JOSEF. 'Kollár vyzývá Šafaříka k rozhodnému vystoupení proti Štúrově separatismu.' *Časopis Musea království českého* (Prague), LXXXVII (1913): 292-3
VOTRUBA, FRANTIŠEK. 'Ľud v bernolákovskej a v štúrovskej reforme.'
*Literárnohistorický sborník* (Bratislava), vol. VI/VII (1949/50): 47-71
VYVÍJALOVÁ, MÁRIA. 'Alexander Rudnay a slovenské národné hnutie.'
*Historický časopis* (Bratislava), XVI (1968), no. 2: 208-30
- *Bernolákov autentický slovníček spred roku 1790*. Bratislava, 1969
- *Juraj Palkovič (1769-1850)*. Bratislava, 1968

- 'Kollárov list z roku 1825 o Čítanke so slovakizujúcimi tendenciami.' *Slovenská literatura* (Bratislava), XIII (1966), no. 3: 271-80
- 'Novšie poznatky k Bernolákovmu Slováru a jeho predhovoru z roku 1796 a 1825.' *Historický časopis*, XVI (1968), no. 4: 475-522
- *Slovenskje Národňje Novini: Boje o ich povolenie.* Martin, 1972
- 'Snaha slovenských vzdelancov založit' katedru na peštianskej univerzite roku 1824.' *Historický časopis*, XVII (1969), no. 2: 218-32
- 'Snahy o jazykové zjednocovanie v dvadsiatych rokoch 19. stor. a Ondrej Bošáni.' *Historický časopis*, XIV (1966), no. 2: 251-63
- 'Snahy o založenie slovenských novín a časopisů tridsiatych rokoch 19. stor.' *Historické štúdie* (Bratislava), VI (1960): 121-67
- 'Spolok milovníkov reči a literatúry slovenskej.' *Biografické štúdie* (Martin), I (1970): 53-68

VYVÍJALOVÁ, MÁRIA, ed. 'Palkovičov preklad Platónovho dialógu v bernolákovčine.' *Literárny archív* (Martin), VIII (1971 [1972]): 7-22
- 'Snahy slovenských vzdelancov o rozvoj spisovného jazyka v 18. storočí a v prvej polovici 19. storočia.' *Historické štúdie*, XIV (1969): 237-50

WAGNER, FERENC. *A szlovák nacionalizmus első korszaka.* Budapest, 1940

ZAY, KÁROLY. *Protestantismus, Magyarismus, Slawismus.* Leipzig, 1841
ZLATOŠ, ŠTEFAN. *Písmo sväté u Bernolákovcov (Juraj Palkovič a jeho slovenský preklad biblie).* Trnava, 1939
ZOCH, CTIBOH. *Slovo za slovenčinu.* Ed. Ivan Stanek. Bratislava, 1958
*Zora* (Buda). 4 vols. 1835-40
*Zpráwa o ústawu slowanském při ewangelickém lyceum w Prešporku na rok 1837/8 wydaná.* Bratislava [1838]

ŽÁČEK, VÁCLAV. *Cesty českých studentů na Slovensko v době předbřeznové.* Brno, 1948
- *Čechové a Poláci roku 1848.* Vol. I. Prague, 1947
- *Z revolučných a politických pol'sko-slovenských stykov v dobe predmarcovej.* Bratislava, 1966
ŽATKULIAK, J.G. *L'udovýchovny pracovník Juraj Fándli.* Bratislava, 1951

# Index